YoungWriters 2006 Poetry Competition

"I have a dream
children will one day
where they will not be judged by the
color of their skin, but by the content
of their character."

Martin Luther King

I have a dream

words to change the world

- MOTIVATE your pupils to write and appreciate poetry.
- INSPIRE them to share their hopes and dreams for the future.
- BOOST awareness of your school's creative ability.
- WORK alongside the National Curriculum or the high level National Qualification Skills.
- Supports the *Every Child Matters - Make a Positive Contribution* outcome.
- Over £7,000 of great prizes for schools and pupils.

"When I was out there I was never ever
alone, there was always a team of people
behind me, in mind if not in body."

Ellen MacArthur

North East & North West England

Edited by Angela Fairbrace

 Young**Writers**

First published in Great Britain in 2006 by:
Young Writers
Remus House
Coltsfoot Drive
Peterborough
PE2 9JX
Telephone: 01733 890066
Website: www.youngwriters.co.uk

SB ISBN 1 84602 654 7

Foreword

Imagine a teenager's brain; a fertile yet fragile expanse teeming with ideas, aspirations, questions and emotions. Imagine a classroom full of racing minds, scratching pens writing an endless stream of ideas and thoughts . . .

. . . Imagine your words in print reaching a wider audience. Imagine that maybe, just maybe, your words can make a difference. Strike a chord. Touch a life. Change the world. Imagine no more . . .

'I Have a Dream' is a series of poetry collections written by 11 to 18-year-olds from schools and colleges across the UK and overseas. Pupils were invited to send us their poems using the theme 'I Have a Dream'. Selected entries range from dreams they've experienced to childhood fantasies of stardom and wealth, through inspirational poems of their dreams for a better future and of people who have influenced and inspired their lives.

The series is a snapshot of who and what inspires, influences and enthuses young adults of today. It shows an insight into their hopes, dreams and aspirations of the future and displays how their dreams are an escape from the pressures of today's modern life. Young Writers are proud to present this anthology, which is truly inspired and sure to be an inspiration to all who read it.

Contents

Kimberley Walton (12)	27
David Spereall (13)	28
Dillan Thompson (14)	29
Ciar Purser (14)	30
Patrick Stead (14)	30
Stuart Watson (14)	31
Millie Myers (14)	31
Paul McGee (14)	32
Rachel Bell (13)	33
Jessika Lousie Morgan (14)	34
Jack Price (12)	34
Sarah Charlton (14)	35
Claire Hepper (14)	35
Alexander Hunter (14)	36
Rachel Knight (14)	37
James Murray (15)	38
Emma Charlton (14)	38
Mark Delaney (15)	39
Sarah Mitchell (11)	39
Toni Redpath (12)	40
Callum Taylor (12)	40
Ben Carvey (12)	41
Laura Nickson (12)	41
Olivia Haile (12)	42
Michael Noble (12)	42
Sally Wheelhouse (15)	43
Rachel Musgrave (14)	43
Lauren Blakeburn (14)	44
Graeme Toppin (12)	45
Philippa Peall (12)	46
Rebekah Ellwood (12)	47
Andrew Clifford (14)	48
William Jones (15)	48
Matthew Largey (15)	49
Hannah Pritchard (14)	49
Justin Sims (15)	50
Laura Howley (14)	51
Emma Jane Bantleman (15)	52

Greenbank High School, Southport
Natalie Tomlinson (13)	53

Joseph Swan Comprehensive School, Gateshead

Knowsley Hey Comprehensive School, Huyton

Malbank School & Sixth Form College, Nantwich

Millfield Science & Performing Arts College, Thornton Cleveleys

Parkside Comprehensive School, Willington Crook

Lauren Edge (13)	76
Nicola Evans (12)	77
Owen Heslop	78
Benjamin Trotter (11)	78
Sarah Akers	79
Liam Allinson	79
Rebecca Lyle (12)	80
Oliver Mason	81
Andrew Peacock	81
Rebecca Macdonald (12)	82
Jonathan Ian Marriott	82
Scosha Parker	83
Amber Scott (12)	83
Craig Skidmore (13)	84
Victoria Facey (13)	84

Rydings Special School, Rochdale

Scott Buik (14)	85
Thomas Maiden (14)	85
Callum Brady (11)	86
Kyle Sampson (14)	86
Shahzad Siddique (11)	87
Toni Parker (14)	87
Karen Rowell (14)	88

St Edmund Arrowsmith Catholic High School, Ashton-in-Makerfield

Nathan Hughes (13)	88
Chelsie Kennedy (12)	89
Louise O'Connell (12)	89
Katie Lever (13)	90
Laura Jarmesty (13)	91
Sarah Parkinson (12)	92
Amy Cotton (11)	93
Charlotte Mayes (12)	94

Trinity School, Carlisle

Nicola Curry (12)	94
Lucy Meekley (12)	95
Jack Mallam (12)	95

Hannah Edwards (13)	96
Zoe Blythe (12)	96
Brandon Longcake (11)	97
Rebecca Dixon (12)	97
Abbie Brayton (12)	98
Andi Menzies (12)	98
Dominique Toms (12)	99
Trudi Newgarth (11)	99
Ben Bolton (12)	100
Alex Armstrong (11)	100
Samantha Barker (12)	101
Liam Gilmour (12)	101

Walbottle Campus Technology College, Walbottle

Ashley Fortis (14)	101
Danielle Robson (14)	102
Sean McMahon-Harris (13)	102
Jayde Kennedy (14)	103
Sophie Mansuy (13)	103
Jamie Foggo (13)	104
Carl Gilchrist (14)	105
Christopher Burn (13)	106
Kayleigh Lambert (13)	107
Michelle Hunter (13)	108
Rebecca Pearson (13)	108
Peter Watson (13)	109
Beth Atkin (12)	109
Hollie Slack (13)	110
Sam Kingham (13)	110
Kirsty Forster (13)	111
Amy Lawson (13)	111
Louise Forster (13)	112
Katie Makepeace (13)	112
Rachael Mowat (13)	113
Ross Tweedy (13)	113
James Bennett (13)	114
Craig Baines (13)	115
Georgia Dodds (13)	116
Danny Bowers (13)	116
Amy Rebair (13)	117
Kelly Briggs (13)	117

Bhavini Shukla (13)	118
Stacey Shoker (13)	118
Michael Dobson (13)	119
Sarah Bambrough (13)	119
Paige Temperley (13)	120
Rosul Mokhtar (13)	120
Matthew Summers (13)	121
Chris Shorter (14)	121
Rebecca Foster (13)	122
Stephanie Guy (13)	122
Jonathon Bartlett (13)	123
Aaron Clasper (13)	123
Holly Laws (14)	124
Jake Richardson (13)	125
Daniel Gilbert (13)	126
Connor M Roberts (13)	127
Amy Thompson (14)	128
Megan Armstrong (13)	128
Emma Larrad (14)	129
Sheryl Munroe (14)	129
Rachel Dickinson (14)	130
Jack Routledge (14)	130
Kerry Donnelly (13)	131
Chris Simmons (14)	131
Agatha Kona (13)	132
Samantha Turner	132
Charlotte Fisher	133
Andrew Walker (13)	133
Amy Vaughan (14)	134
Clare Goodwin (13)	135
Claire Packham (14)	136
Peter Ward (14)	136
Gabriella Michelini (14)	137
Rebecca Goodall (14)	137
Andrew Leigh (14)	138
Michael Black	138
Holly Taggart	139
Liam Stewart (14)	139
Robbie Soulsby (14)	140
Gavin Smith (13)	140
Sammiejo Straker (9)	141
James Clark (14)	141

The Poems

I Had A Dream

What is the meaning of war,
Is it guts and gore?
Why do people declare it?
Why can't we all live in peace?
Let's withdraw and cease.

The army says, 'No, no we must fight,
We must fight with all of our might.'
They have a 50/50 chance to live,
But they have to much more to give,

Why do we have to hurt others?
Why can't we treat them like sisters and brothers?
After all there is only one world,
We are all the same
And war is a deadly game.

It seems to be part of the human condition,
That humanity is on a destructive mission,
Can't we change and be more loving,
Conflict can lead to famine and drought,
Nobody understands what this is all about.

Family and friends feel pain in their heart,
When the fighting has to start,
Do these soldiers really want to desert their family,
Or do they have no choice?
Do they want to stay safe at home or go onto the battle dome?

Why can't we just sit down and say
War has had its day,
Today is the day for a new beginning!

Bethany Hayes (12)
Birkenhead High School, Birkenhead

Make Poverty History

No one should live in a shed,
No one should starve,
No one should have nothing,
Poverty should be history.

No one should have no money,
No one should be unhappy for their whole life,
No one should have no comfort,
No one should have no education,
Poverty should be history.

Everyone should have some comfort and happiness in their lives,
Everyone should have good food every day,
Everyone should have good jobs and earn a good amount of money,
People should be like this!
Make poverty history!

Some places like parts of Africa are in poverty,
They didn't choose it,
They didn't choose to have no money,
They didn't choose to not have enough food each day,
They didn't choose to have nothing,
This should be stopped,
So help to make poverty history!

Make poverty history.
This would be my dream!

Rhiannon Frostick (12)
Birkenhead High School, Birkenhead

I Have A Dream

I have a dream,
That one day,
The world will be equal
And each individual's voice will be heard.

I have a dream,
That there will be peace
And a sense of equality,
In every corner of the Earth.

I have a dream,
That war is not known
And kindness
Is the only thing known to man.

I have a dream,
That poverty and abuse,
Are not an option
And that everyone lives in harmony.

I have a dream,
That one day we will be as one
And no one will be alone
And if my secret dream comes true . . .

No Childline, no drug abuse,
There wouldn't be much need for these,
In my perfect world, my perfect world,
My dream.

Catherine Lowther (12)
Birkenhead High School, Birkenhead

I Have A Dream

I have a dream that every child has a life like mine,
That they have food on the table three times a day,
They have a tap with clean water pouring through
And they have a place to call home, which is safe and warm,
A family that loves them, no matter what,
That they have a teacher, to teach them
And books to read
And friends when in need,
Most of all that they lead a life which is full of fun,
Where they can play in the sun and dance in the rain
And they don't have to work and suffer in pain.

This is my dream, it is a very large dream,
But that is the way it is,
I hope one day this dream will come true,
But we will have to wait and see,
I am lucky and so are you, but others aren't as fortunate
As me and you.

I have a dream . . . do you?

India Casey (12)
Birkenhead High School, Birkenhead

I Have A Dream

Dreams are mythical and they won't come true,
But there is always hope that they might do,
So I never stop dreaming for the day,
When cancer will stay away,
Never give up the fight,
Otherwise you will live in fright,
People come and people go,
People live in sorrow,
An end to cancer is not far away,
So don't be in dismay,
I assure you, it will get here one day.

Freya Hassall (12)
Birkenhead High School, Birkenhead

I Have A Dream

I have a dream that countries can live in peace without a
                                        threat of war,
That we can kindly welcome foreigners into our country,
I have a dream that we can go abroad when and whenever we like,
That we can walk into the streets without having to run back
Into our cellars because of the sirens,
I have a dream that men and women, black or white,
Fat or thin can get along,
That we no longer need guns or swords if two presidents argue,
I have a dream that we can stay with our mothers and fathers,
Aunties and uncles, brothers and sisters,
That children can stay with their mothers and fathers
Throughout their life,
I have a dream that children can stay in one school,
That they no longer need to be evacuated to another country
With another family,
This is my dream.

Rebecca Santo (12)
Birkenhead High School, Birkenhead

I Have A Dream

My dream's to get racism kicked out of mind,
It's all in people's feelings, there's nothing to find,
What's the difference between black and white?
What's the point in making a fight?
In sport, the crowd and their racist ways,
For them, their lives are just like a maze,
If you don't like it, why should they?
Differences should be celebrated day by day,
Thin or fat, fat or thin,
It shouldn't matter what country they're in,
With a small amount of support we can make this stop.
Full stop.

Katie Colvin (12)
Birkenhead High School, Birkenhead

I Have A Dream

I have a dream that one day this world will stand up,
Be realistic and face the truth,
I wish that all animals could be free,
Out in the wild - not stuck under a roof,
Animals that are put through pain,
On their way to death and the drain,
Why should they die?
I really ask why - *why?*
They want to live a life too,
Like me and you,
So can we please let them?
Can we let them have comfort, freedom, peace?
We can do much more - but that is just the least.
They do not just die and end up on your plate,
They are tortured, put through pain, this is their fate,
So can we change our selfish ways?
Can we not torture the poor chicken -
Just for the eggs it lays?
So I have a dream,
I have a dream that this world will change the ways in
Which it treats animals because right now - it is *mean.*

And I have a dream.

Chloe Higham-Smith (12)
Birkenhead High School, Birkenhead

My Dreams Of The World

My dream of the world,
Is for all guns to be thrown away,
So that we can unfurl the declaration of freedom
And hope for peace to flow out over all our countries.

These bombs that a few own,
They destroy people's lives,
Why can't governments be shown,
A new way to agree and just
Get along happily?

My dream of our planet,
Is to end all the pain
And ridicule the man that offers
Only war and death.

These knives some own,
Are used for stealing lives,
Then they wait at home,
While they wash the blood off their hands.

My dream of the world,
All in all, is
To kill the weapons that have killed,
To end the raging wars,
To hold hands with our enemies
And most of all to bring peace to our planet.

Ceri-Anne Barrow (11)
Birkenhead High School, Birkenhead

I Have A Dream

I have a dream,
In which we live in peace,
No vandals, the homeless,
Roam the streets.

I have a dream,
In which war doesn't exist,
Men and women are equal,
This law persists.

I have a dream,
No one can be,
Ruled over, pushed down
By humanity.

I have a dream,
Where the world is happier,
God's people aren't bullied
And we live for the better.

My dream won't come true,
The world can't work this way,
Everyone is selfish,
Day after day.

This dream I keep having,
It's real in my head,
It's impossible, hopeless,
Alive in my bed.

So I keep on dreaming,
Of equality and peace,
Help make my dream come true
And help the unfairness cease.

Sally James (12)
Birkenhead High School, Birkenhead

I Have A Dream

I have a dream,
That children can enjoy school,
That they can look forward to it
And be happy with life as a child.

Some unfortunate children can't,
Because they are tormented by someone: a *bully*
For a stupid reason!
But that stupid reason will still get them down.

They don't have the inner strength to stand up,
To stand up and say, 'No,'
If only they knew,
That the bully is a coward,
Nothing more.

I have a dream,
That children can enjoy life again,
That they don't worry at night about the next day,
That they can actually stand up and say no,
Not simply imagine themselves doing that.

But I want that dream to become reality.

Constance Batterbury (12)
Birkenhead High School, Birkenhead

Racism

I have a dream that we . . .
Yes, you and me,
Black or white

Could work, live and grow up together,
Yes, together,
Through life or death.

We shall put our hearts together
To win,
Yes to win the battle
And to succeed.

No matter what happens or what we do,
We, together as a team,
Will find the joy and hope,
To stand up against all,
Those in favour
And win.

To tell you the honest truth,
We have arms and legs
And so do they,
We also have a face,
With a nose, mouth and eyes
And so do they.

We have families,
So do they,
We have hopes, dreams and beliefs,
So do they,
What more can we say
Except stand up for what you believe
And shout, shout from the rooftops
I believe.

Chloe Senogles (12)
Birkenhead High School, Birkenhead

I Have A Dream That We Should All Live Fairly

I have a dream that in this world,
The hopes of men shall not be curled,
Up in a ball, in a corner, just there,
Because that's not right, that's not fair.

I have a dream, that far-off tribes,
Will be strong enough to decline bribes,
Of permission to take their land and life
And slash away at their dreams with an anxiety knife.

I have a dream that Third World farmers' living
Will be respected and loved as they're so forgiving,
That things such as fair trade will win in the end
And the lives of the rainforest souls will amend.

I have a dream that fairness and hard work will win,
Over problems like selfishness, cruelty and sin,
These people deserve more than they get,
Their dreams and aspirations need to be set.

I have a dream that big companies will go down
And they'll not be able to clown around,
Then they'll see that this is no joke,
Like the lives of the people they did provoke.

I have a dream that we all are the same,
That both life and living are not a game,
We only get one chance at being us,
Let them gain and achieve, let them live *fairly!*

Antonia Karus-McElvogue (12)
Birkenhead High School, Birkenhead

Bullying

They throw a ball at me rather hard,
I scream for help, they push me to a wall,
I moan and groan, no one cares,
They try to throw a chair at me,
I stop this from happening, they laugh in class about me,
They call me mean names,
I always lean forwards although they still hit me,
I go home moaning and groaning,
Always finding it hard to compete against them in class.

They are always hitting me,
I always think I should stop kidding myself,
I have always felt heartbroken,
I have tried speaking to a teacher,
But I doubt they will find out very soon,
I have always wondered whether I have done the correct thing,
I can't stop thinking about what is going to happen to me next . . .
I have always felt very sad,
I do try to talk to my dad about this.

I find a way to talk to people about this,
This can't be easy at all,
I have tried calling Childline,
They couldn't help me,
I finally found a way that the bullies would stay away from me,
The best way is to stay out of their way.

They keep coming near me,
How can I stop this?
I try to talk to my dad,
I feel very scared although . . .
It was the best way to stop this . . .
Why can't bullies just get along with other people?

If you are bullied, don't let it carry on,
Think once,
Think twice,
Go and tell the teacher or your parents now!

Petina Liu (12)
Birkenhead High School, Birkenhead

Smoking

Smoking should be banned,
She's throwing her life away,
She thinks it's really cool,
But I think it's really not!
She doesn't know the truth,
That if she keeps it up,
She will be lying on her own,
In a hospital zone.

You see smoking is the cause for cancer,
Whether we like it or not,
She should read the signs on the boxes,
Because they do have a meaning,
It really pains me to say this,
But millions of people die each day,
So if she keeps this habit up,
She will be joining those millions,
On their deathbeds.

The problem is the government,
The people are all hooked,
But the price you pay,
For what I call 'killing sticks'
Goes to the men in black suits.

We need to stop this now,
For our great nation will fall.

Isobel Berry (12)
Birkenhead High School, Birkenhead

Bullying Poem

If you have ever been bullied you will understand what
 I am trying to say,
Just think of those poor children who fear their school day,
Every day is torture, every night is full of fears,
Every time they walk into school, they want to burst into tears,
They can't think about anything fun,
But they don't have the courage to tell anyone,
They feel no joy, only despair,
Being bullied is just not fair,
When you next see a bully,
Make sure you understand fully,
Just what the victim is going through,
Don't just stand there being glad it isn't you,
I'm telling you this to make you aware,
Of how much bullying goes on out there,
So next time you see a child in despair,
Go and comfort them to show them you care.

Evelyn Roberts-Jones (12)
Birkenhead High School, Birkenhead

Am I Scarred . . .?

Everybody hides from me,
Nobody's my friend,
It's a horrible sight to see when . . .
Even my own kind, hide from me in the end.

People live in a place,
Where everybody's got their back,
But when I try to tie my lace,
I get hit in my back.

How can your skin cause you so much grief?
You're always edgy and always scared,
When it's really down to your belief,
Now I believe I'm truly scarred . . .

Aakansha Pandey (12)
Birkenhead High School, Birkenhead

I Have A Dream

I have a dream that everyone will be friends,
Until the very end,
For people to love and care for one another,
People to cherish their feelings to every other,
Everyone to think of others,
Not just themselves,
It doesn't matter how children or adults look,
It is the inside which counts.

I have a dream that everyone will act the same,
To think about what they are going to say before they speak,
If you don't like it, why would they?
I believe that this racism can stop.
Full stop!

Christie Shillinglaw (12)
Birkenhead High School, Birkenhead

I Have A Dream: The Iraq War

I have a dream,
To end the war in Iraq,
Of death, bloodshed and destruction,
Of fear, terror and sorrow,
Lives shattered, wasted,
By grenades, landmines, bombs,
The people dying through no fault of their own,
Their screams,
Their pain,
Shall be heard forever,
But why don't we stop this,
Shall we stop this together?
Shall we stop this now?

Helen Corlett (12)
Birkenhead High School, Birkenhead

I Have A Dream . . .

Day by day, our world is getting destroyed by the slithering
Snake of global warming,
Our icebergs melting as the hiss pass by,
Our animals dying as the snake licks its lips.

I have a dream to stop this,
No burning hot sun to burn our Earth,
No enormous icebergs melting like snowmen,
No animals being only a whisper of the past.

This dream can create a world free of global warming,
Then our sun can relax and blaze on our Earth calmly,
Watching our animals playing on the solid, freezing ice.

Sophie Yates (12)
Carmel RC Technology College, Darlington

My Dream Is To Travel The World

My dream is to travel the world,
To travel all over the globe,
To learn about different cultures,
To see different creatures.

To see different things,
To see different foods,
To speak a different language
And to taste a different sandwich.

I dream of stopping animal cruelty
And changing the world, ending poverty,
This really is a novelty.

Hannah Parsons (13)
Carmel RC Technology College, Darlington

Dreams

Every person has a dream of what they want to be,
Of what they want to do
And what they want to see.

People's dreams can change their lives
If they come true,
They want to be original,
They want to be brand new.

Some people dream of stopping world hunger,
Or making women look a lot younger.

Imagine a world without a worry,
But that won't happen in a hurry.

If only, if only dreams would come true,
Let's hip, hip, hooray when they finally do.

Laura Edgar (13)
Carmel RC Technology College, Darlington

Peace Dream

There is endless pain and suffering,
That really needn't be,
If everyone loved each other,
Then we all would see,
That the world is a better place,
When people get along,
When we start doing right,
Instead of always doing wrong,
Few of us do something
And just care about ourselves,
We ignore the cries of others
And ignore children's yells,
If only we could end this living hell.

Michael Boylan (13)
Carmel RC Technology College, Darlington

Dreams Of Rock

Me and my band,
Called 'Undersided',
Dream of rocking the world,
Like McFly did.

We like to be different,
Stand out from the crowd,
Acting arrogant, eccentric
And being loud.

Making friends with Green Day,
And Blink 182,
Taking after Nirvana,
Also U2!

Performing in front,
Of loads of fans,
Unlimited shopping,
Tour with the band!

Changing the world,
With our hard-hitting lyrics,
We don't want to be like,
A rock band gimmick!

We dream of writing,
Performing too
And trust me,
We will rock you!

Megan Alexander-Weir (13)
Carmel RC Technology College, Darlington

My Dream

My dream is to change the world,
To make it a better place,
When I walk down the street,
I dream everyone will have a smiling face.

My dream is to find true love,
They should treat me the way I deserve,
Buy me flowers, perfume, expensive gifts,
Or just truly mean it when they say 'I love you!'

My dream is to save a life,
It could be an animal of some kind,
It may be small, but at the end of the day,
I know I've made a difference to mankind.

My dream is to erase world poverty,
Just to give a starving child bread,
It may be a tiny contribution,
But is it better for them to be alive or dead?

Everybody has a dream,
To be a doctor, nurse, sing or dance,
The question is are dreams possible?
The answer is yes, as long as you take the chance.

Amy Parkes (13)
Carmel RC Technology College, Darlington

Piano Keys

Black, white, what's the big thing?
We're all people whether we're thick or thin,
What's the problem, we're practically the same,
We walk, we talk, we eat and sleep,
We're all alike in some ways.

Bad thoughts, good thoughts,
They are hardly alike,
The quarrelling goes on,
They argue all night,
One doesn't mind them, the other complains,
'I want them out,' the other's OK.

The piano keys, they are black and white,
But they should like one million colours in our minds,
They are the lyrics to a song I know,
A song I know, never to be heard.

One day I wish, one day I have a vision,
One day I have a dream, for equality,
For fairness among humanity
And peace amongst the races.

Liam Slade (14)
Carmel RC Technology College, Darlington

I Wish

I stand at the bus stop,
Dreading the other kids coming,
My life, I hate,
My life, I wish was over.

On the bus I sit,
Kids teasing, laughing,
All aimed at me.

In school I sit,
Crying out for help,
I hate bullies,
I hate teachers,
I hate myself!

I wish this would stop,
I wish,
I wish,
Maybe my wish will
Come true one day,
Maybe today!

Riah L'Estrange (14)
Carmel RC Technology College, Darlington

I Dreamed A Dream

When I dream a dream at night, I dream of many things,
I may be a bird flying high with my feathery wings,
I dream of everything I want in my own vision,
Doing tests and getting top marks without any revision,
I dream of travelling around the world,
Or walking down the catwalk with my hair curled.

I dream of no more slave trade,
Having to work all day without really being paid,
No more world poverty,
Wouldn't it be a novelty,
I dream of world peace too,
No more diseases, no more flu.

Wouldn't it be great to have so much money,
Or sit around and eat toast and honey,
I think of all the many jobs,
Being a policewoman and catching yobs,
Wouldn't good weather be so nice,
I've only seen the sun once or twice.

Emma Bartram (12)
Carmel RC Technology College, Darlington

Spokesperson

We need a spokesperson to help our cause,
To make the listeners hear and pause,
It would take one voice in the crowd,
To say what's wrong and speak aloud,
To speak out against racism everywhere,
It is as though no one dare,
To disagree with terrorism all over,
From Baghdad, Kashmir or the white cliffs of Dover,
Someone to say equality is unjust,
It is that person we will follow and trust,
To say nothing matters like colour and creed,
A spokesperson for the world, that's what we need.

Nick Baldwin (14)
Carmel RC Technology College, Darlington

My Dream

I want to be a footballer and play in Spain,
The first time down the tunnel to play the game,
Hear the crowds roar go round and round,
I get my first touch, it brings me to the ground,
If I score, it's an extra pound,
I boot the ball towards the net,
It's going in, do you want a bet?
It goes in and hits the ground,
Now I've earned my extra pound,
People are looking at me like I'm Steven Gerrard,
Or are they thinking that I'm Frank Lampard?
I've always wanted to be these people,
Now my dream has finally come true.

Phillip Park (13)
Carmel RC Technology College, Darlington

I Have A Dream

Gunshots fired,
Grenades thrown,
Big explosions,
Soldiers groan.

Will war end?
No one's sure,
Everyone's on rations,
Because they're poor.

How did it start?
Someone gets hurt,
Dive for cover,
Stay alert.

If war ends,
The world will be greater,
No more hatred
And put a stop to the dictator.

James Butterfield (13)
Carmel RC Technology College, Darlington

Life Would Be Better If . . .

Life would be better if everyone was happy,
Wouldn't it be Heaven if you could walk along in peace,
No worries, just calm,
People chattering about nice things,
Instead of about how life is unfair,
Life would be better if everyone was happy.

Life would be better if everyone was friendly,
A wave at the old lady across the road,
Instead of a nasty glare,
No thugs attacking the innocent at night,
Instead, helping them with their bags,
Life would be better if everyone was friendly.

Life would be better if people were supportive,
They congratulate you when you achieve your goals,
Whether they are pleased or not,
When you are down, they give you a smile
And a word of friendly advice,
Life would be better if people were supportive.

You can change the world if you just try
And make a person's day,
Be kind and friendly and supportive too,
If only to your friends each day.

Francesca Brown (13)
Carmel RC Technology College, Darlington

My Dream

I had a dream about the World Cup,
And for once, England weren't fed up,
They got to the final with Brazil,
A game we'd win, I believed we will.

The game kicked off and I was in the crowd,
Brazil scored first and the fans went loud,
But we quickly equalised with a great goal,
From England's finest: Joe Cole.

At half-time, the scores were level,
A goal from Rooney, set up by Neville,
But Ronaldinho skinned the defence,
2-2, the game was getting tense.

As the game entered injury time, we all began to sing,
When Aaron Lennon ran down the wing,
He crossed it to Rooney, who hit it first time,
In the back of the net, the goal was fine.

We sang, we danced, we rejoiced together,
As England got to keep the cup forever!

Harry Miller (13)
Carmel RC Technology College, Darlington

My Dream

Some people dream of being rich,
I do,
Some people dream of being famous,
I do,
But I know it may not happen.

My dream is to help stop poverty,
Create a community,
Some people have nothing, are nothing,
Mould their lives and make them new,
That's the dream I'd like to fulfil.

Some people have a dream job,
I do,
Some people dream of travelling the world,
I do,
But I know it may not happen.

My dream is to stop war,
Have peace throughout the world,
No more guns, no more bombs,
No more deaths, no more mourning,
That is the dream, which I wish to happen!

Jessica Furphy (13)
Carmel RC Technology College, Darlington

Violence

I have a dream there will be no more violence,
No more fighting on the streets,
The world will be a better place,
No more people crying in fear,
No more people getting in trouble,
No more guns pointing in your face,
The world will be a better place.

Lewis Metcalfe (12)
Carmel RC Technology College, Darlington

I Have A Dream

K ick racism out of life,
I t's the main source of war and strife,
C olour of skin is not important,
K ick racism out of life.

R acist people,
A ttack each other,
C ontent of character,
I s what's important,
S o fight for your freedom of speech, as
M artin Luther King once did.

O ut with suffering, in
U nderdeveloped countries they should not be
T reated differently.

O bjects are material possessions and aren't important,
F ighting is *not the answer*!

L ove thy neighbour, the Bible says,
I t hopes for a lasting peace between nations,
F ree of wars and disturbances where,
E veryone gets along with one another!

Kick racism out of life!

Jordan Hickman (13)
Carmel RC Technology College, Darlington

I Have A Dream

People who care will get their fair share,
People who don't won't,
People who spread the word,
Shall be heard,
People who smile as bright as the sun will have fun,
Everyone is responsible in their own way
And I dream that some day all the
Bad people in the world will pay!

Kimberley Walton (12)
Carmel RC Technology College, Darlington

For The Sake Of Everybody's Dream

On the 11th September 2001,
Many seen alive, were found to be gone,
As America's greatest buildings were felled,
The distraught survivors came together and gelled.

From out of nowhere came the plane,
To destroy the buildings and inflict pain,
For America, this was no gain,
That day there was no sun, only rain.

Osama bin Laden owned up to the attack,
While America's security was found to be slack,
Afghanistan became the victims of invasion,
It seemed for no one there was elation.

A few years later, tragedy struck again,
Not in America, but this time in Spain,
Hundreds of people, blown up on a train,
Yet more agony and yet more pain.

Victims' families were understandably distraught,
With protests, words and action they fought,
Against a world of terrorism, which has to be stopped,
But then again, out of nowhere, terrorists popped.

London was bombed, many people died,
Though we must fight on against this tide,
Of terrorism that goes on our planet,
For the sake of people let's ban it.

We are human beings, we have human rights,
To live and to die with no frights,
So terrorists abandon your explosives and guns,
For the sake of your children, your daughters and sons.

David Spereall (13)
Carmel RC Technology College, Darlington

Drought

The mud is dry and so are the mouths of villagers,
It has not rained for ninety days, the well has dried,
The ground cracks and winds like a maze with no end,
We walk and walk to seek some water
But the roads keep winding and bending as you walk into
                                                    the hazy mist.

The vultures circle waiting for a weary victim to fall,
This I really hate,
The dried bones are a constant reminder
Of how much water we have
And each day our villagers sing, dance and pray,
For our most desirable delight - water.
When the sun rises and it chases shadows to
Their chilled comforts, it begins to fall down
And huge booms and crashes commence,
This we know is what we longed for,
The rain has come, we thank our gods for this day,
It rises high, it bursts its banks,
Now we give our god great thanks for this glorious wet day.

Dillan Thompson (14)
Carmel RC Technology College, Darlington

No More War

A world without war would be great,
When eating dinner off my plate,
On the radio I hear reports,
Of the soldiers lost at war,
The world would be a nice safe place,
Without war at our door,
Now in the world more are hurt
And left there lying in the dirt,
Some are dead,
Some have bled,
I think of them when lying in bed,
I hope the world will end in peace
And all the soldiers will retreat
And police won't have to be on the beat,
If the world was safe, it would be great,
When eating dinner off my plate.

Ciar Purser (14)
Carmel RC Technology College, Darlington

Pollution

Smoke billows from the chimney,
Like an old man on forty a day,
Kills all of the ducks and the birds of prey,
Kills all the fish and sharks,
Even the dogs with the annoying barks,
Kills all the cattle and sheep,
Leaves them in a stinky heap,
The polar ice caps will melt,
The sea level will rise,
Floods all over,
Millions will die,
The planet will heat up to a high,
Watch all the people,
In the astonishing heat fry.

Patrick Stead (14)
Carmel RC Technology College, Darlington

Third World Freedom

I have a dream that there aren't Third World countries,
But people go through this daily,
They walk for miles to a well,
Without food their stomachs swell,
Children are born with HIV,
This lifestyle doesn't appeal to me,
Standing all day in the sweltering heat
And relying on charity-earned meat,
To live without rain in the dust
And get along some days with only a bread crust,
The flies swarm around their eyes
And it isn't unusual if a baby cries,
We should raise money for a cause that is true
And be like soldiers to the rescue,
Something to help must be done
And make these people's lives more fun.

Stuart Watson (14)
Carmel RC Technology College, Darlington

Dreams Of A Shadow

I have to go to school today,
I hate the girls that make me pay,
They say they're superior,
That they're the best,
They claim to stand out from all the rest,
They make me feel oh so small,
Whilst they are standing six feet tall,
They talk to me like I'm not there,
Sometimes I wonder, why do I care?
Because these girls can't ruin me,
That's a fact,
They're bossiness is just an act,
But I'm better than them
And I know that!

Millie Myers (14)
Carmel RC Technology College, Darlington

My Dream About Pollution

Pollution is in the air,
Pollution is on the ground,
Pollution is all around.

Pollution makes the world look bad,
Animals die, people cry,
People sad, we look bad.

It only takes one voice,
One voice in a crowd,
Could that voice be you?
Could you make the whole world proud?

Why do we litter?
It only makes us bitter,
Why don't we recycle?
It makes the world less frightful.

Could you stop pollution?
Could you be that voice?
Could you be a better human?
Could you be that voice?
Could you save the next generation
From living in pollution?
Could you be that voice?

All you need to do
Is stand up for what is right,
Stand up to pollution,
Stand up to a baying crowd.

Stand up for the world,
Make the whole world proud.

Paul McGee (14)
Carmel RC Technology College, Darlington

Why Is There Pollution?

Why is there pollution?
I can tell you why.
Just carry on reading this poem
And you will find out why.

Pollution is created by:
Litter on the streets,
Chemicals in the seas
And many more things.

So, how can we stop it?
You just need to,
Stop feeding the land and sea,
Full of bad things.

Instead of this you could,
Recycle your litter,
Bin your litter,
But don't drop your litter.

If you stop littering,
Our world that we live in,
Could be a cleaner,
Pollution-free zone.

Rachel Bell (13)
Carmel RC Technology College, Darlington

Fancy Waking Up One Day

Fancy waking up one day,
Without the sound of birds,
But the sound of running water,
The sound of crying floods your ears.

Fancy waking up one day,
Having your whole life changed,
All the memories of your life,
Drowned in the muddy sewage.

Fancy waking up one day,
Wanting to change the world,
Stop the flooding water,
Prevent the air pollution.

Fancy waking up one day,
Knowing you changed the world,
You stopped the muddy flood,
Fancy waking up one day.

Jessika Lousie Morgan (14)
Carmel RC Technology College, Darlington

There Will Be Peace

Violence happens everywhere,
People fighting like dogs in the street,
Or beasts killing on the plains of the globe,
Let's all get together and be bold,
Lay our weapons on the ground and
Live in the joy of a perfect world,
Send erroneous people to a faraway land,
Prevent crime and racist abuse,
For the people on the receiving end,
It is like being on a separate land,
Stop dictators in their tracks then . . .

There will be peace.

Jack Price (12)
Carmel RC Technology College, Darlington

Terrorists

The eyes peer over the dark, black mask,
Those beady, hungry eyes,
The man, he stops just along the road,
While grinning all the while.

His jacket full and padded,
His grip tight and strong,
As he grips his jacket pocket
And continues through the throng.

Twenty minutes later,
I heard a sudden beep,
People running and screaming,
Along the crowded street.

That towering inferno,
The blazing pit of hell,
I watched the total horror
And others did as well.

I glimpsed a sight so awful
And since I felt the pain,
Because since July 7th,
Things will never be the same.

Sarah Charlton (14)
Carmel RC Technology College, Darlington

I Have A Dream

I have a dream,
Anger will no longer be in people's lives,
Happiness will be the only important thing,
The views of everyone will be listened to,
Except for the people who want to hurt others,
Wars will never happen, the world will finally be at peace,
The pollution that threatens to wipe out the entire population
Will be stopped and we will all put our minds to
                                    solving the problem,
Maybe one day this dream will come true.

Claire Hepper (14)
Carmel RC Technology College, Darlington

My Dream Of Power

It won't last forever,
All this stuff won't,
We take it all for granted,
The things we need most.

Oil and coal,
We need for power,
For the simplest tasks,
Like taking a shower.

But we use these too much,
We're running out fast,
We can't go for much longer,
Like we could in the past.

We've thought of alternatives,
Like nuclear power plants,
But that's far too dangerous,
It's destroying our planet.

We could use steam,
But that's not very fast
And this is the 21st century
And steam's in the past.

There is also solar panels,
But in England, they're effect is small
And what about in the winter?
You could have no power at all.

However wind power is perfect,
With these huge turbine machines,
So wind power is the future
And wind power is my dream.

Alexander Hunter (14)
Carmel RC Technology College, Darlington

My Dream

Look deeper in and you will see,
Bullies aren't always what they're meant to be,
Because just sometimes in your world,
Your own best friends can be the girls,
The very ones who tease and hit,
The very ones who taunt and spit.
And it's not right, and it's not fair,
How you make fun at me, laugh and stare,
Because if you truly were my friend,
You'd want to make my misery end
And now I fear coming to school each day,
For fear of which new taunts you will say
And I wonder if you think it through,
Of all the things you're about to do,
Because every single living day,
Your harsh sharp words take me away,
Do you know how much they sting?
And have you noticed the marks on my skin?
Have you noticed the smile gone from my face,
My distant looks as if I'm in another place?
Sometimes for moments you are fine
And for a second, I can smile,
Then again it all comes lashing out
And I just want to scream and shout,
All the while, I smile and nod along,
Whilst wondering what really have I done wrong?
Because you see you're bullying me
And I am stupid because I cannot see,
So next time you think to hurt this girl,
Just think and wonder, what if this was your world?

Rachel Knight (14)
Carmel RC Technology College, Darlington

I Have A Dream . . .

I have a dream . . .
Of a place where terrorism doesn't exist,
Of a place where all Asians aren't blamed for terrorist acts,
Of a place where people trust each other and are not wary,
Of a place where your skin colour doesn't make you a target.

I have a dream . . .
Of a place where it's safe to go out at night,
Of a place where our kids can play and be safe,
Of a place where pensioners are at ease in their own homes,
Of a place where we can live without fear.

I have a dream . . .
Of a place where starvation and famine don't return every year,
Of a place where AIDS and disease don't kill thousands,
Of a place where there are no wars between countrymen,
Of a place where people, animals and crops can survive.

I have a dream . . .
    Of an ideal world . . .

James Murray (15)
Carmel RC Technology College, Darlington

I Have A Dream

That everyone will do their fair share to save the planet,
From the toxic waste and the steaming, rising temperature,
The fuel prices will continue to soar like there's no end,
Till we realise what we're doing.

I have a dream that this world will continue to grow
And build up the strength to override this pollution of the world
And that we learn how to help ourselves by doing
A little easy thing, like walking.

If we try to act more then the changes we make
Will shine in years to come,
I have a dream that the world, because of our changes,
Can be the perfect and ideal world.

Emma Charlton (14)
Carmel RC Technology College, Darlington

I Had A Dream

To understand peace is to solve arguments,
Cruelty and war, to help environments, poverty and more,
Without peace there wouldn't stand a tree with dust
And ash as far as I can see,
We build weapons to kill instead of helping the ill,
But with peace they will,
With peace you'd gladly give money
And then you'd understand fully,
That you can help evade death,
By giving someone an extra breath,
No war, no poverty, no cruelty,
With peace and serenity and feeling free,
We can help the homeless and those in distress,
I had a dream, here is a piece,
I had a dream, it ended in peace.

Mark Delaney (15)
Carmel RC Technology College, Darlington

I Have A Dream

I have a dream,
That may seem,
Impossible to some people.

But not me!

I want friendship across the world,
No wars, no fighting or abuse.

I want love and care and agreement,
Across the many nations.

I want people to work together
And stop all that racism.

I want bullies to go extinct,
Or turn into nicer people.

I want a lot for all this fighting to stop,
But that is my one and only dream.

Sarah Mitchell (11)
Carmel RC Technology College, Darlington

Can You Change The Meaning Of Life?

When I have dreams,
No one else can see them,
Are you wondering what my dreams could be?
On my left, poverty and hunger,
On my right, cancer and AIDS,
We need cures, we need money,
Others need it more,
We can laugh, we can sing,
But they can't move for famine and drought,
These people need help,
Think how it would feel,
Suffering, agony and torture,
Anguish, fear and bloodshot eyes on faces as black as death,
So make my dreams come true,
So the world can be a better place,
For me and for you.

Toni Redpath (12)
Carmel RC Technology College, Darlington

Imagine

Imagine if there were world peace,
Oh wouldn't it be wonderful,
No war, no violence, no bloodshed, no pain,
Imagine, imagine, no guns, no knives, no bombs,
                              no grieving mothers,
Imagine,
Everybody happy, smiling,
Having fun,
Imagine, imagine,
All countries united together in love and harmony.

Callum Taylor (12)
Carmel RC Technology College, Darlington

I Have A Dream

I have a dream,
That people will stop polluting the planet,
I have a dream,
That there will be no more high tides,
I have a dream,
That the sea levels will stop rising,
I have a dream,
That animals' habitats will be reclaimed,
I have a dream,
That the ozone layer will stop intensifying,
I have a dream,
That we will stop global warming,
What a dream!

Ben Carvey (12)
Carmel RC Technology College, Darlington

I Have A Dream . . .

My dream would change the world forever,
It would be to have a cure for every disease,
Which would put the NHS at ease,
It would put a smile on everyone's face,
It would make the world a better place,
Deadly illnesses would be no more,
People wouldn't have scars that would be sore,
Needles would be forgotten, so would the flu,
Which would be a loss in the sales of Kleenex tissue!
So imagine that world, what do you see?
A much happier world for you and for me.

Laura Nickson (12)
Carmel RC Technology College, Darlington

I Have A Dream

I have a dream,
A dream where there isn't global warming,
Like a world filled with flowers,
All love
And no things changing.

I have a dream,
A dream where there isn't any wars,
Like a world filled with peace,
All happiness
And no fighting.

I have a dream,
A dream where there are no illnesses,
Like a world full of health,
All smiles
And no sadness.

Olivia Haile (12)
Carmel RC Technology College, Darlington

I Have A Dream

I have a dream,
That people will stop being racist,
I have a dream,
That people will not destroy human and animal habitats,
I have a dream,
That people will stop polluting the planet,
I have a dream,
That animals don't get killed by humans,
I have a dream,
That there will be less poverty and no people
Lying on the streets without sleep, food and drink.

Michael Noble (12)
Carmel RC Technology College, Darlington

I Have A Dream

I have a dream that world peace will arise,
    Those terrorists will die,
    The earthquakes will stop
    And the buildings will no longer drop.

I have a dream that the seas will stay calm,
    That no more tsunamis will dawn,
    The icebergs won't melt
    And the ships will no longer sink.

I have a dream that the extinct animals will still be here,
    That the animals won't be killed for fun,
    Those creepy crawlies will crawl away to the depths of Hell
    And that we are all immortal.

Sally Wheelhouse (15)
Carmel RC Technology College, Darlington

I Have A Dream

I have a dream,
The world will be a better place,
That people won't invade each other's space
And harm the human race.

If only the shooting and bombs would stop,
Then the world would not have to stop.
Then the soldiers would get a better job,
So their parents would not have to sob.

To be a soldier is not a sin,
To want to see your next of kin.
To live in hope and not in fear,
To live a dream for everyone here.

Rachel Musgrave (14)
Carmel RC Technology College, Darlington

I Have A Dream

I have a dream,
That one day everyone can walk together,
In rain or shine, whatever the weather.

I have a dream,
Where there is no colour discrimination,
Where the world is joined as one nation.

I have a dream,
Where everyone is friends
And for that friendship to never end.

I have a dream,
Where everyone is free,
Where no one is treated differently.

I have a dream,
Where there is no war,
Where fighting foes should be no more.

I have a dream,
That could go on for days,
Just for everyone to change their ways,
I have a dream . . .

Lauren Blakeburn (14)
Carmel RC Technology College, Darlington

I Have A Dream

Say yes to recycling,
You know it's correct,
Say no to greenhouse gases,
Or the world will come to an end,
Say yes to planting more trees,
It takes away all the gases,
Say no to pollution,
Otherwise we will die,
Say yes to trying to prevent flooding,
Or there will be destruction,
Say no to always using your car,
They give off fumes that can kill you,
Say yes to saving electric,
Or we won't have any in the future,
Say no to nuclear power,
The fumes harm us all,
Say yes to energy-saving equipment,
Because we will survive,
Say no to dropping litter,
It makes the world unclean,
Say yes to preventing global warming,
You know it's correct.

Graeme Toppin (12)
Carmel RC Technology College, Darlington

I Have A Dream

I hear the sounds of war,
See the blood,
The darkness.

I've known the destruction of people,
Felt the trees,
The pain.

Now I have a dream,
The candle bright,
Banishing darkness.

The world joins hands,
Black and white,
All friends.

No more sounds of war,
No more blood,
Only light.

No more destruction of people,
No more tears,
Only happiness.

My voice spoke out of the darkness,
'Stop the wars,
Bright light.'

Now all the world joins hands,
Black and white,
All friends.

Everyone,
Together,
As one.

Philippa Peall (12)
Carmel RC Technology College, Darlington

I Have A Dream

I have a dream,
To make the world better for everyone,
The rich, the poor, the old, the young
And generations later on.

A cleaner environment, no waste chucked in the sea,
People who are caring, kind, full of generosity,
I want free speech, where everyone's opinion can be heard,
Good things, bad things, anything, let them spread the word.

Let's make an end to poverty,
Let's fight back to disease,
Let's look after the Earth
And we'll get along with ease,
Stop the crime and the wars,
Life is only short,
Later, when the Earth is better,
You'll wonder why we fought.

Most of this, can be achieved,
As hard as it may seem,
But if we all just work together,
I'll no longer have to dream.

Rebekah Ellwood (12)
Carmel RC Technology College, Darlington

I Have A Dream

I have a dream that global warming,
Can be reversed, no need for warning,
We can use our cars without any worry,
But everyone will still be in a hurry.

I have a dream that war will go
And like a river, peace will flow,
No shots will fire, no deaths occur
And the peace they share will never stir.

I have a dream that disease will go
And stop, die and let health flow,
That a cure for all disease is found
And stops people hitting the ground.

I have a dream that crime will go
And big criminal businesses will not flow,
Some people are scared to go out,
Because they know they'll get mugged without a doubt.

Andrew Clifford (14)
Carmel RC Technology College, Darlington

I Have A Dream

I have a dream that war is at peace,
That the guns have stopped to say the least,
The battle is over, the destruction has ended,
Death is leaving and the injured are being mended.

I have a dream that global warming,
Can be stopped before the end starts dawning,
The burning sun, the harmful rays,
Have disappeared until the end of days.

The end of war and global warming,
These should occur without warning,
The killing will end and all will flow free,
This is my passion, this is my dream.

William Jones (15)
Carmel RC Technology College, Darlington

I Have A Dream

I have a dream that clear water
Will once again flow in the streams.

I have a dream the litter of rubbish will
Be replaced by the litter of leaves in the cold winter months.

I have a dream that clouds of pollution
Will be replaced by white clouds of purity.

I have a dream that the chimneys of industry
Will fall as the great pine trees do now.

I have a dream the fish will once again
Swim in the sea as they did before
The disease known as pollution hit.

I have a dream the pollution will stop
And the environment will rebuild itself.

Matthew Largey (15)
Carmel RC Technology College, Darlington

I Have A Dream

Change the world and recycle.

Rubbish, rubbish everywhere,
Do people really care?
Plastic bottles, paper, tins,
Why can't people put them in bins?

Homeless people on the streets,
Sleeping on seats,
While we endlessly think of ourselves,
New clothes galore,
Do we really need more?

Lots of trees are getting cut down,
If we recycle less rubbish goes into the ground.

Change the world and recycle.

Hannah Pritchard (14)
Carmel RC Technology College, Darlington

A Dream Of No More School

Test after test,
They give me no rest,
I hate to revise,
It wears out my eyes,
Please Almighty God,
No more rotten school.

That would be great,
More time with my mate,
There wouldn't be another test,
Loads of time to have some rest,
I would play football in the sun,
That would be a load of fun.

All the teachers would be fired
And my eyes wouldn't be so tired,
There wouldn't be any GCSEs
And to everyone that would please
And if the school was to be killed,
All my dreams would be fulfilled.

But to school I must go,
That is so low,
At school I get a load of pain,
Because tiny is my brain
And since this is a dream,
I can't forget the standard scream.

Justin Sims (15)
Carmel RC Technology College, Darlington

I Have A Dream . . .

I have a dream to make the world a better place,
To abolish poverty and world hunger,
To organise the largest fundraiser in the world
And make the world believe they can do great things,
Such as donating a small sum of money to save a life.

If the world helps, they can prevent AIDS and
                              premature death in Africa,
They can prevent the pain and suffering that they go
                              through every day,
Because if we don't act and show them we care,
They will suffer even more
And then the world will become a terrible place.

Africa is like a desert of despair,
But we are here to help until the end,
Because it is people like us that make the world go round
And because of what we say and give,
It makes the world a better place to live.

Live 8 is the concert that changes the world,
With its contribution and many fans that attend,
Many bands like U2 and Green Day,
Can change lives with a single performance,
Because of the heart Bob Geldolf has.

I have a dream to make the world a better place,
If I had the chance, I would achieve all the goals I set above,
Because no one deserves to live in poverty and despair,
I would also contribute toys and clothes and food,
Because they have been through so much
And deserve something special.

Laura Howley (14)
Carmel RC Technology College, Darlington

My Dream Is For My Father

I have a dream,
That the world is a better place,
Anger and fear has melted away
And madness has no trace.

The guns that show their fates,
Have now been deeply buried,
As the soldiers arrive at the Pearly Gates.

It's about safety and song
And a life that has no need to worry,
Nothing would ever be wrong,
Good people wouldn't have to suffer.

Time for light and hope to take over,
Trying to stop the fight,
Spreading faith around the world.

My dream is for my father,
Because then he wouldn't have to fight,
He would be safe and tucked up tight,
Then I wouldn't have to be scared,
That my father won't be there.

Emma Jane Bantleman (15)
Carmel RC Technology College, Darlington

I Have A Dream

I have a dream,
I said to myself,
But it's not to be famous,
Or to come into wealth.

My dream is amazing,
But one day you'll see,
We'll change the world,
Just you and me.

Many heroes have passed by,
Have helped us to stay,
As the civilised nation,
We are today.

The people we admire,
Who've helped those in need,
They have created,
The lives that we lead.

But wherever there's war,
Or people who need assistance,
We'll be there to help,
Despite our resistance.

So my dream is,
To save our generation,
To carry on humanity,
To form a congregation.

Natalie Tomlinson (13)
Greenbank High School, Southport

Who I Admire

My mam and dad,
Are whom I admire,
To be with them forever,
Is what I desire.

They love me so much
And I love them,
My family is together,
Like paper and pen.

Sometimes we shout
And our hearts fall,
But together we know,
That we are a whole.

There's days when I'm out
And I'm not there,
But it doesn't matter if I'm gone,
We will always care.

Our love for each other
Is very strong,
We are going to be a family
For very long.

When we all die,
My family of seven,
We will meet up
And live happily in Heaven.

Katherine Kennedy (12)
Joseph Swan Comprehensive School, Gateshead

I Have A Dream

I have a dream,
Of a world without war,
That the fighting will stop
And we all follow the law.

I have a dream,
Of a world without hate,
Without death and destruction
And everyone's your mate.

I have a dream,
Of a world without greed,
Where people don't want more
And no one's in need.

I have a dream,
Of a world without terror,
Where we respect each other
And we're all together.

I have a dream,
Of a world without smoking,
A world without pollution,
Causing a national choking.

I have a dream,
That one day this will all be real,
That the wars will end,
Making this dream real enough to feel.

Nathan Newton (13)
Joseph Swan Comprehensive School, Gateshead

I Have A Dream

My father, my father,
Is there when I'm hurt,
To drive me to the hospital.

My father, my father,
He said to me,
He got the best
Birthday present in the world,
I was born on his birthday,
Got the same name
And we look the same.

My father, my father,
Helps me when I'm down,
Picks me up when I'm down,
My father, my father.

Just say he is my dad
And my friend is my dad,
He helps me out when
Things are tough.

But at times things
Are not very good
But it's my father
That cheers it up.

My father, my father,
I am him,
He is me,
My father, my father,
Is my heart and soul.

James Burns (13)
Joseph Swan Comprehensive School, Gateshead

Beauty Shop

I have a dream,
To own a shop,
You can come to me,
If your hair needs a chop.

The blusher and lipstick,
The scissors and the dye,
When my clients are beautiful,
I'll wave them off goodbye.

Manicure and pedicure,
I will also do,
Absolutely any colour,
From the range of pink to blue.

When people need their hair done,
I'll make it look nice,
They will be satisfied with their hair
And even ask for some advice.

So that's my shop,
It's not time to close,
This is the dream I have,
When off to sleep I doze.

Megan Moody (12)
Joseph Swan Comprehensive School, Gateshead

The World

I have a dream,
I dream to stop pollution,
Pollution that could kill us all.

I have a dream,
To stop people from smoking,
Or it will be your fault,
When you are choking.

I have another dream,
To stop all wars,
What's the point when there is no cause?

I have another dream to fulfil,
To stop people using drugs,
If we don't, who will?

I have another dream,
To stop all crime,
But we'd better hurry up,
We're running out of time.

My second to last dream,
Is to make recycling proper,
So go and recycle your copper.

My final dream,
Is to make everything right,
So go to bed and turn off the light.

Carl Shanks (13)
Joseph Swan Comprehensive School, Gateshead

I Have A Dream

My dream is to have a beauty shop,
Not to slave away with a duster and mop,
I love the glam and glitzy things,
Diamonds, rubies and the other blings,
Beauty and make-up is what I do,
Manicures and pedicures sometimes too,
I make people look like stars,
They can strut their stuff in the bars,
People will often praise me,
Say I am fantastic,
But all I would have done is make them look like plastic,
My shop will put the glam in glamour,
But I will keep in a sophisticated matter,
One of these days I will be a beauty queen
And that is my amazing dream.

Sarah McKeough (12)
Joseph Swan Comprehensive School, Gateshead

Everton Legend! Gone!

Duncan Ferguson, Everton born, Everton bred,
Football was the way he was led,
He played most of his career at his favourite club,
After each game he would enjoy a pint at the pub,
He will always be remembered as a great,
If you want to watch him, you are too late,
He was idolised by all the fans,
Although throughout his career he receives lots of bans,
Sadly he has left and gone,
After all those years he has shone!

Jake Acklam (14)
Knowsley Hey Comprehensive School, Huyton

My Inspiration

Sirens sound in the middle of the night,
Blazing lights through the blinds,
Bangs on the door,
I cry for help,
Footsteps and the door swings open.

'Help!' I scream. 'He's hurt his head!
We need to get him to a hospital bed.'
They put him on a stretcher
And carry him down the stairs,
I hold his hand all the way,
'Don't let go!' I hear him say.

My eyes fill up as we climb abroad,
Thinking about the mess I've caused,
Racing through the deserted roads,
As tears are steaming down my face,
'It wasn't your fault,' he reassures me,
'It was, it was,
I'm so sorry!'

It finally stops and the doors fly open,
They pull him out and wheel him in,
I follow frantically running in
Into a room, they take him in a hurry,
I stand outside, my head full of worry,
I stand by the window gazing through,
Looking at the caring doctors he's with,
Makes me feel lucky these people are near,
Now I know there's nothing to fear.

For all of you who practice in medicine,
Everyone should know you deserve a medal,
This is what inspires me
And that is what I plan to be.

Zoë Brannan (14)
Knowsley Hey Comprehensive School, Huyton

Extraordinary People

Hugs and tears from family and friends,
Will they come home alive or dead?
They wish them luck as they go off,
In the green and brown camouflage,
These soldiers are on a mission for us,
To protect us from a world of mistrust.

In their destination they have arrived,
What their eyes witness will stay in their mind,
Fear and pain among young and old,
The most torturous thing they will ever behold,
These men and women are faced with death,
But their passion burns on, this is what they do best.

They have been spotted, they don't know it yet,
One's the next name on the list of the dead,
His finger's on the trigger,
He's pulled it now,
Argh!
The shrieks are deafening, he falls to the ground.

The troops fall silent,
Their eyes filled with tears,
They have taken away what was not rightfully theirs,
A man, an inspiration,
To all young or old,
Who fought for their lives to lose his own soul.

Amy Forrester (14)
Knowsley Hey Comprehensive School, Huyton

I Have A Dream . . .

I am writing this poem on what I want to be,
When you have read it,
You will see that one person who inspires me.

When I grow up I want to be a star,
I want to be famous,
I want to go far.

I want to be like Marilyn Monroe,
She is the one person who inspires me so,
She could act
And she could sing,
Marilyn could achieve anything.

She was the face of Chanel No 5,
She is still remembered,
Although she's not alive.

Marilyn was so confident,
As you grow to be,
She started off so ordinary,
Just the same as me.

She fulfilled her life to the most,
Because she really cared,
She got what she'd always wanted,
She got what she deserved.

For I would like to be like her,
As hard as it may seem,
But all I have to do from now,
Is simply follow my dream.

Louise Keating (13)
Knowsley Hey Comprehensive School, Huyton

I Have A Dream

What do nurses do?
What do they see?
They help sick people including me.

They would like far more time to sit by you and talk,
They bathe and feed you and help you to walk.

Nurses love to hear of your lives
And the things you have done,
Your childhood, your husband and your son.

Nurses are people with feelings as well
And when we're together you'll often hear tell
Of the dearest old gran in the very end bed
And the well-known grandad and the things that he has said.

They feel your pain and know of your fear
That nobody cares now your end is so near
And help the young children who are in need of some help
And provide the love and care towards them as well,
If you cut your knee,
Or bang your head,
You'll soon be in a hospital bed.

This is my dream to become a nurse,
I hope my dream doesn't come to an end.

Faye Hathaway (14)
Knowsley Hey Comprehensive School, Huyton

My Inspiration

I hear you ask, who inspires me,
To this I answer simply,
The person who inspires me most,
Deserves to have a champagne toast.

So many words to describe this inspiration,
She would give her life just to please a nation,
With her words of wisdom and loving caress,
All the wounds I gain she would dress.

Loving and caring while I go through battle,
Not minding cage, those I would rattle,
She overcomes obstacles placed in her way
And carries on her life straight away.

So, in case you're wondering who my poem is about,
I'd hate for you to feel any more doubt,
This poem is about a person stronger than any man,
Obviously this poem is about my nan!

Ashley O'Neill (14)
Knowsley Hey Comprehensive School, Huyton

My Baby Soldier

In the wars of Iraq,
They rarely need a medi-pack,
England and America stick together
And hopefully will do forever.

We will use the Royal Navy,
For the protection of our baby,
The man you see who walks with the gun,
Just happens to be my baby son.

If your son goes to Iraq,
Please hope to God he will come back,
Awaiting news, I really dread,
Could my son really be dead?

Paul Healy (14)
Knowsley Hey Comprehensive School, Huyton

A Tale OF The Heroes

Men and children had to leave their families,
Most wouldn't return or become casualties,
They had to fight in World War I and II,
Most of the children were the same age as me and you.

They fought and lived in the trenches,
Even if there were dead bodies and horrible stenches,
The living conditions were a disgrace,
Especially when grenades blew up in your face.

Your commander yelled over the top,
Men ran and you saw the bodies drop,
Soldiers ran across the battlefield,
With no protection, armour or shield.

They would get to the other side,
But this was like suicide,
You'd either get stuck in barbed wire and die,
Or reach the German trench and get shot in the eye.

It had all started from one man,
Everyone thought no person can,
Murder an innocent six million Jews
And be so cruel as to rob their clothes and shoes.

And when the war was won and over,
These brave soldiers sailed back to Dover,
They returned to their families,
To tell of their experiences and their memories.

Lewis Jefferies (14)
Knowsley Hey Comprehensive School, Huyton

Unlikely Inspiration

Whilst you think of famous people who inspire you,
Have you ever spared a passing thought for those around you too?
Almost every day you see them, they greet you with a smile,
I've noticed they're an inspiration, why did it take me such a while?

What a wonderful thing to be able to do,
Share all of your knowledge and be a friend too,
Helping to make your near future more bright,
Telling you that you should be more polite!

Always willing to help you learn,
Looking after you with greatest concern,
Friendly and helpful, always willing for a laugh,
This you can say about all teaching staff.

Whenever you need a helping hand,
Just ask one of my teachers, they'll understand,
They'll help you do it, to finish the work,
Whilst being there to make sure you don't start to shirk.

If you're feeling a bit upset,
You can talk to the teachers so don't sit and fret,
They'll sort out your troubles and help calm you down,
For this on its own, don't they deserve a crown?

They set you your targets and help you achieve,
Tell you that in order to do it, in yourself you must believe,
They set your mind in your work, say, 'Follow your dreams!'
They treat people equally, never choosing teams.

So next time you're looking for inspiration like me,
Just think for a minute of those who every day you see,
The people who teach and give their knowledge to you,
My teachers are inspirational: don't you think that it's true?

Matthew Marshall (14)
Knowsley Hey Comprehensive School, Huyton

I Have A Dream

I have a dream that everyone will have food
And that everyone will have enough water,
That they will all live a life that's full,
Education as an option,
A family that's around,
Someone to love them
And to care for them,
Enough money,
A good job,
We can dream.

Anthony Hockenhull (13)
Malbank School & Sixth Form College, Nantwich

Dreams

I dream of a place,
At the back of my mind,
Nothing can hurt me,
Where people are kind.

I dream of a world,
Beyond the stars,
There is no terror,
No fumes and cars.

I dream of a universe,
Away from all war,
Earth melts away,
I close the door.

It is just a dream
And it makes me feel blue,
But believe in your dreams,
They may just come true!

Rachel Allen (12)
Millfield Science & Performing Arts College, Thornton Cleveleys

I Have A Dream . . .

That people solve their problems with words, not bullets,
And don't solve their differences with nuclear bombs.

I wish people wouldn't fight over races and colour,
Those who start wars don't think about the people,
Who have bombs dropped on their houses.

My message through this poem is:
We have neglected the world through war and pollution!
Wouldn't it be better if people solved their problems civilly,
As Churchill said, 'Jaw, jaw not war, war.'
We should follow these words!

Laurence Beer (12)
Millfield Science & Performing Arts College, Thornton Cleveleys

Racism

We don't need racism,
We need kindness,
People get bullied,
Because of their race,
They shouldn't get picked on,
For the features on their face.

White and black people are the same,
We're in this world to play the same game,
People get shot by bullets so hot,
Does it matter the colour on their face?

When it's time to leave this place,
When hopefully racism is tamed,
Let's do it as one human race.

Joanna Olive (12)
Millfield Science & Performing Arts College, Thornton Cleveleys

I Have A Dream!

I have a dream,
To banish racism in the world,
When I see someone being racist,
It makes me want to cry,
But it makes other people want to die.

I want to banish war,
It makes me want to roar,
I want to shout and scream,
But when I wake up, it's all been a dream.

I had another dream last night,
Where people didn't fight,
Oh I wish it was real,
Instead I hear people squeal.

But I guess I will have to carry on dreaming,
Because people still are screaming.

Natalie Bird (12)
Millfield Science & Performing Arts College, Thornton Cleveleys

I Had A Dream

I had a dream, the world was perfect,
No racism, no hate nor fate,
There was love and we all rose
To Heaven above,
No fighting or biting but smiling
And writing poems of friendship,
Where people did not care if you
Were black or white, light or heavy,
It was what was inside that counted,
No rubbish was mounted on streets
And there was no poverty in Third World countries.

Sam Tempest
Millfield Science & Performing Arts College, Thornton Cleveleys

No Solution

What is a dream?
A fantasy,
With a beam of light,
Leading you to peace.

I had a dream once,
A world with no bad,
A place of freedom,
And I was so glad.

But who would listen to a child's dream,
Or theme?
No one,
No one.

A world of life,
Is a world of peace,
But no place is perfect,
And that's no excuse.

The world won't reflect,
On things that have happened,
Like bombers, murders,
Or even assassins.

When a country is hit,
The only cause is revenge,
It's like a game of tag,
With no start or end.

Luke Treece-Birch (12)
Millfield Science & Performing Arts College, Thornton Cleveleys

Problems

Countries need to help everyone,
When some don't hopes are just, gone,
When we have lives in our hands,
We have to think about how desperate people are
To cockle on Morecambe sands.

We need to help or countries will crumble,
There'll be more problems, the country will stumble,
Enough about the problem, what about the solution?
Less car use is the solution to pollution.

There's many other problems to think about,
But enough solutions? I very much doubt,
There's poverty and global warming,
In Africa, diseases are swarming.

There was a famous speech, 'I have a dream.'
We need to help, work as a team,
A couple of problems are racism, knives and guns,
But problems are everywhere, they come in tonnes.

Solutions are coming, but very slow,
Indeed they're coming but we need to go, go, go,
We need to hurry up and help everyone whatever the race,
But what a reward to see the smile on their face.

Micheal Barrett (12)
Millfield Science & Performing Arts College, Thornton Cleveleys

My Dream

The world is full of green trees,
No pollution in sight,
There's so little destruction,
No one wants to fight,
No cars on the roads,
Only buses and bikes,
All the kids eating healthy,
Exercising each night.

All the people are equal,
All treated the same,
The young and the old,
From wherever they came,
People feeling happy,
Animals are tame,
Even winning doesn't matter,
Cos it's only a game.

It's great on the beaches,
Water blue and so clear,
The people are tidy,
No litter around here,
No hunger or murder,
Everyone is so true,
To aid and to help
Is what people will do.

This might not be real,
These things are not seen,
This isn't reality,
It's only a dream.

Ben Redman (12)
Millfield Science & Performing Arts College, Thornton Cleveleys

Equality

Sprung is a trigger,
A bullet to the head,
A detonated bomb,
Finishes the dead.

A clash between nations,
Where desolation roams,
A meaningful silence,
Can be heard through the groans.

Along came starvation,
Followed by hurt,
And then by warfare
A bloodstained shirt.

A blast with explosions
Only based on revenge,
A sick mind at work,
That we can't comprehend.

The everlasting heartache,
Is starting to end,
Through the copious grieving
And round the next bend.

Sam Butler (12)
Millfield Science & Performing Arts College, Thornton Cleveleys

A Situation

A situation of fighting people,
People using racism for violence, it is hell,
Can people really stop it?
Just stop this war!
I wish people would carry on like they used to,
People helping each other like they used to.

Michael Gorse (12)
Millfield Science & Performing Arts College, Thornton Cleveleys

Different

I'm in a black hole that I call my world,
I'm the same as them if my hair's straight or curled.

Small things like hair colour, on that I'll turn my back,
But when people make fun because people are black.

Or have a different religion or have a problem with their speech,
I want to change the world, I want to teach.

The world's about being equal and about a different race,
Not to be cruel to people because of the colour of someone's face.

I wish the world would wake up and see,
That people destroy humanity for them and for me.

Kate Taylor (12)
Millfield Science & Performing Arts College, Thornton Cleveleys

The Thought In The Back Of My Mind

I have a thought in the back of my mind,
Sometimes it gets so hard to find,
I see homeless children wandering the streets,
Just wanting to be loved, no shoes on their feet.

Does it matter the colour of my face?
This is my home, a dark black space,
Walking miles for a sip of water,
Saying goodbye to my ill dying daughter.

Why do these white people get treated better than me?
This little thought in the back of my mind,
What can I do to make you see?

Alice O'Neill (12)
Millfield Science & Performing Arts College, Thornton Cleveleys

I Have A Dream

I have a dream
That people will put a stop to racism
Leave the victims alone when they have done nothing wrong.
Treat them how you want to be treated
By other people.

I have a dream
That bullying will stop
Cowards will go away.

So come along
Back me up
Don't just sit there
Like a pup
Think of all the people that are sad
Because someone has done something
So bad!

Matthew Allan (13)
Parkside Comprehensive School, Willington Crook

I Have A Dream

I have a dream that everyone is
friends no matter who they are.

I have a dream that everyone stands
up and speaks, even if they are alone.

I have a dream that everyone who
has something bothering them
tells someone else and that everyone
helps each other.

I have a dream that even if people
think that something is good,
people will still try to make it better.

James Crawford (12)
Parkside Comprehensive School, Willington Crook

I Have A Dream

I have a dream about the world,
It's nice, it's good, it's new,
It's something to inspire me,
It's something to inspire you.

It helps me think of all the things that people wish to do,
It gives me something to write about when I'm feeling blue.

I will help people no matter what,
They're just people like me,
They've done nothing wrong.

Their skin may be black,
Their skin may be white,
But no matter what they will be God's creations for life.

So why say things to hurt them in any way?
Because, they're ordinary people at the end of the day.

I also had a dream that the sky started to bloom,
It no longer was a beautiful misty silk,
Nor a fresh sky-blue.

It was now a clogged up sky,
Full of colourful flowers,
Not much to look at, at all,
Not something to admire

Just a mix of different colours,
Jumbled in a ball,
Some people could admire it but not me at all.

Then all of a sudden my dream went away,
I finally woke up,
It was a brand new day.

Lauren Edge (13)
Parkside Comprehensive School, Willington Crook

The Imagination Of Everyone's Souls

The imaginations of everyone's dreams are different
in every way,
The small things in life really help the Third World countries,
The way we think, the way we speak, each person judges
us with their pride and ego,
Each person is different, with the colour of their skin or their race,
Everyone is a jewel with a singular shine, a work of art
with their own rare design,
Everyone's bodies, minds and souls are the same but all in
different ways,
I dream about the day when all of the sins that we have done will
be erased in the future and we will all live in peace and happiness,
I know that everyone's hopes are combined with the beauty of the
past and all the best hope in the future,
Dreaming is where you are in charge of what happens,
People may tease you but we are all the same in minds,
bodies and souls,
Discovery is when people venture into the secret world and beyond,
There is another world that people don't see,
The mysterious goings on that we don't realise are there,
Your boundless energy can take you anywhere in the world,
You own individuality is like a path that unwinds your future,
Your pride is like a bird with out-spread wings,
Wouldn't it be awesome to make a breakthrough into
another secret world?
When you open a book you open your entire mind,
If you don't take action your mind floods with fear,
When you believe in yourself you believe in everything you do,
Don't be bullied by someone older, take action straight away,
Friendship, when you make a friend, you are a friend for life,
Follow your heart and try to follow all of your ambitions that
you would like to do in life,
Nothing grows in the same way twice.

Nicola Evans (12)
Parkside Comprehensive School, Willington Crook

I Have A Dream

I have a dream that poverty
Is like a washing machine
The dirt goes away and never will stay
I just wish poverty will go away.

Black and white, what's the difference?
It's like cat and dog, they hate each other
Come on everyone, love one another.

War and death, it's all around
Like grass and trees
You never can miss it
It makes me cry, it makes me sad
War and death is really bad.

Children are like china dolls
You have to wash, clean, love and care
Not throw them away
And pretend they're not there

I hope my dreams all come true
I hope this nightmare will soon be through
Please cruel world, let them go
Stop this never-ending show.

Owen Heslop
Parkside Comprehensive School, Willington Crook

My Dreams . . .

D on't have to die
R elief from all pain
E veryone happy and free
A ll illnesses cured
M eat, we don't have to eat
S uffering at an end.

Benjamin Trotter (11)
Parkside Comprehensive School, Willington Crook

I Have A Dream

I had a dream I was on my own.
I was lonely with no friends.
I tried to make friends but no one listened.
In my dream I cried at night.
I cried myself to sleep.

Don't bully people!
Treat people how you would like to be treated!
Treat people with respect and make more friends!

Other people are just like you . . .
If someone bullied you
You wouldn't like it
Remember that!

You wouldn't bully someone because of blonde hair,
So don't bully people for the colour of their skin . . .
Or if they are a good student
Bullying is a sign of jealousy . . .
Just remember that if you are a bully.

One day the person who you bully will turn around and bully *you* . . .

Sarah Akers
Parkside Comprehensive School, Willington Crook

My Dream

I have a dream
A dream of peace
And quiet
A dream of happiness
Where I can make black people
And white people the same
I dream I can clear all poverty.

Liam Allinson
Parkside Comprehensive School, Willington Crook

I Have A Dream

The dream that I have is to help change the world,
To stop racism and stop people who are abusive.
I would like to stop cruelty to animals and also to kids,
But please make sure you keep on your lids!
Don't be angry, don't be mad,
Because you may make many people sad.

I would like to change the world,
And help bullied people.
People who get bullied may show no pain,
But deep down inside they are hurt and feel like a tiny sand grain.

My dream of a new world would be totally changed.
A change that only we can change.
Where people say hello in the morning,
And where people say goodnight in the evening,
Without any pain.

Also, I would like to change the way people treat each other.
You should not treat people the way you treat your brother!
You should treat people the way you would like to be treated,
Don't blow your tops like a fire being heated!

The world I think about is where everyone is kind,
Where you see people who are different to you,
And you don't mind.

So come and help me
Try to change the world.
But before you do that,
You must change yourselves.

Rebecca Lyle (12)
Parkside Comprehensive School, Willington Crook

I Have A Dream

I have a dream
That poverty is like a machine
It gets old, goes slow
Then goes away.

I have a dream
That poverty is a dream
It vanishes every day
Just like a dream.

I have a dream
That parents give their children ice cream
Not hurt them
And make them scream.

I have a dream
That people never starve
People are starving
I hope their dreams come true.

Oliver Mason
Parkside Comprehensive School, Willington Crook

I Have A Dream . . .

We should have world peace and stop fighting
with other people in the world and remain as
we are with land we own, nobody should have
to fight for their country.

Use less petrol so there is little pollution.
I want no racism; it is your personality that counts.

I have a dream that bullying will stop
and the cowards who use bad language will shut up and pop.

We should give people our food and love because they are poor
and need our help.
So be the one to change their lives forever.

Andrew Peacock
Parkside Comprehensive School, Willington Crook

I Have A Dream

I have a dream
That we all live in peace, all different nations for we are
all God's creations
I have a dream
That war is all over. I wish that wish on a four-leaved clover
I have a dream
That animals are not ignored and people don't leave them
to suffer when they get bored.
I have a dream
That hunger is not an option; poor people will smile
in their own satisfaction.
I have a dream
That the bullied no longer live in fear because they are scared
to go to school, they think the end is near.
I have a dream
That we can make a difference, we can help and care
We can sort out all of this mess people have made
We can slay off this madness
We can save the day.

Rebecca Macdonald (12)
Parkside Comprehensive School, Willington Crook

Dreams

D reams are whatever you want them to be
R is for how really wonderful dreams are
E is for everything you can imagine
A is for the attitude of people in the world if they dreamed more
M is for more things that could come true
S is for the amount of sadness in the world until everyone
    follows their dreams.

Jonathan Ian Marriott
Parkside Comprehensive School, Willington Crook

Dreams

I had a dream in the night, the world was kind,
The world was bright,
All the people were friends, smiled once then smiled again,
God was happy, the Devil was sad,
I heard a noise that I didn't like, the children cried for their lives,
The noise I heard was something bad, I walked to the crow to see
a flag,

The civil war had broken out,
I wanted to scream, I wanted to shout,
But no words were coming out of my mouth.

The war ended but the world was not the same,
People did not smile, people had changed,
I thought to myself, *what can I do?*
Can I change the children's ways?
Then I woke up and it was the very next day.

Scosha Parker
Parkside Comprehensive School, Willington Crook

I Have A Dream . . . To Stop Animal Cruelty

They have no voice, so who can hear?
The poor little animals live in fear,
They're smacked and slapped and kept alone,
And taken away from what they thought was home,
There are some people who can help.
They hear cats cry and dogs yelp,
But sometimes they ignore this cry
And leave without even a goodbye.
If you ever hear this call,
Tell someone who can help.
Silence the animals' yelp!

Amber Scott (12)
Parkside Comprehensive School, Willington Crook

A Dream

In my dream
There would be no racism
No poverty
And no war

Everyone would have equal opportunities
But no one would be the same
It wouldn't matter if you were black or white
You would be treated the same

If everyone was the same
The world would be boring
You would learn nothing new
That's what my dream would be.

Craig Skidmore (13)
Parkside Comprehensive School, Willington Crook

Dreams

Dreams are important
Dreams are exciting,
Dreams are special,
And are with you for life.

Do you have a dream?
I have a dream,
I think everybody should have a dream.

If you did have a dream
What would it be?
My dream is to help others.

Victoria Facey (13)
Parkside Comprehensive School, Willington Crook

I Have A Dream . . .

I would end all wars,
Smoking would be banned everywhere,
Everyone would have a job,
No one would get ill anymore
And all cars would run on water.

I have a dream . . .
All houses would use solar energy.
No one would have guns anymore.
Every pupil would have their own computer
We would work in the morning at school
And have fun activities in the afternoon.

Scott Buik (14)
Rydings Special School, Rochdale

If I Have A Dream . . .

If I have a dream . . .
Smoking would be banned,
I would make all rich people work in Africa
And donate at least £1 million,
I would put more police on the street
To protect the good people
And everyone would have a smile on their face.

If I have a dream . . .
The sun would shine every day,
Joy riding would be banned,
I would make it rain in Africa to end the drought,
No one would have guns
And there would be no more poverty.

Thomas Maiden (14)
Rydings Special School, Rochdale

I Have A Dream . . .

I would ban people from smoking.
I would ban people from swearing.
There would be more police walking the streets
To make them a safer place.
I would have more peace throughout the world
And I would make it rain in Africa, to end the drought.

I have a dream . . .
I would make every country speak the same language.
I would make sure that every house had its own sweet shop.
All schools would have a five a-side football pitch.
I would make the largest swimming pool in the world
And I would make sure that everything is free.

Callum Brady (11)
Rydings Special School, Rochdale

I Have A Dream

I have a dream that
I will ban joy riding
End all wars
There will be no more poverty
Smoking is banned everywhere
No one to have guns
No one ever goes hungry
And there will be no more child cruelty
Rich people will give money and work in Africa
It will rain in Africa to end the drought
And there will be no more animal cruelty.

Kyle Sampson (14)
Rydings Special School, Rochdale

I Have A Dream . . .

I have a dream that no one will joyride,
There will be a football pitch in every school,
All children will be healthy eaters
There will be no teachers in school
And all cars will run on water.

I have a dream that smoking will be banned everywhere,
PS2 games will be served for only 18-year-olds,
There will be free ice cream for everyone whenever they want one,
There will be free entry into Alton Towers
And shops will never close.

Shahzad Siddique (11)
Rydings Special School, Rochdale

I Have A Dream . . .

If I have a dream . . .
There would be no more poverty anywhere,
There would be peace throughout the world,
Rich people to give money and work in Africa,
All cars run on water,
Smoking would be banned everywhere,
There would be no more child cruelty.

If I have a dream . . .
The world would speak the same language,
Schools become nightclubs after 7pm,
Grown-ups have to do all the jobs,
Summer holidays would last for 12 weeks
And everybody would have a smile on their face.

Toni Parker (14)
Rydings Special School, Rochdale

I Have A Dream

If I have a dream . . .
No one would get ill,
The shops would never close,
All the children would enter the X-Factor competition,
There would be peace all over the world
And I would make sure that Burnley won the Premiership.

If I have a dream . . .
There would be PE for everyone, even the grown-ups,
Everyone would have water in their homes,
There would be no more mosquitoes,
Every day the sun would shine
And I would get married to Robbie Williams!

Karen Rowell (14)
Rydings Special School, Rochdale

I Dreamed A Dream

The team was here ready for action
To win the game would be true satisfaction
The crowd was singing, the crowd was wild
My childhood dream since a child
The game had started, the tackles were tough
The opposition manager was shouting in a huff
The whistle blew we were halfway there
Opponent fans were in for a scare
The end was near, we could sense the win
But at the last minute here players grin
The whistle went, the team had won
They got the trophy, problem was it weighed a ton!
The biggest upset in rugby history
Would it be beat a true mystery?

Nathan Hughes (13)
St Edmund Arrowsmith Catholic High School, Ashton-in-Makerfield

I Dreamed A Dream (About My Mum)

I had a dream about my mum
It wasn't sad, it wasn't glum.
My mum is cool, my mum is fun,
She always seems to know everyone.

My mum has really trendy clothes
This is something that everyone knows.
She paints her nails and paints her toes
Wherever she goes she always glows.

I will love my mum forever
We will always be together.
All through spring and all through winter
Forever and ever and ever and ever.

Chelsie Kennedy (12)
St Edmund Arrowsmith Catholic High School, Ashton-in-Makerfield

I Dream A Dream

I dream a dream
Of somewhere far away,
I dream a dream
Of somewhere warm to stay.

I dream a dream
of somewhere close and near,
I dream a dream
Of somewhere I don't fear.

I dream a dream
Of somewhere no one else knows,
I dream a dream
Of somewhere calm where it snows.

I dream a dream
Every night,
I dream a dream
What will it be about tonight?

Louise O'Connell (12)
St Edmund Arrowsmith Catholic High School, Ashton-in-Makerfield

I Dreamed A Dream

I love my dreams
They are a part of me
Without my dreams
I cannot see
Because they are a part of me!

My dreams are cool
Cos they make me think
Especially when the boys wink!

I dreamt one night
About a terrible sight
Where flames soared high
In the night sky!

Then a person came to me
A red devil is what I see
The flames go higher up the sky
Till I burn with heat inside!

As I choke
I hear a croak
Of my mum calling to me!

I finally wake
To find my mum looking down on me!

I love my dreams
They are a part of me
Without my dreams
I cannot see
Because they are a part of me!

Katie Lever (13)
St Edmund Arrowsmith Catholic High School, Ashton-in-Makerfield

I Dreamed A Dream

I dreamed a dream
Although it seems
Things were all so weird
Most of them things I've always feared

Spiders and heights
Gave me so many frights
I just wanted to scream
Please be a dream, just please be a dream

I screamed and I screamed
I wanted to die
I wanted to fly
Away in the sky

The light turned on
I was awake
My mum was there
What was that scream?
That was a dream
The night I dreamed a dream!

Laura Jarmesty (13)
St Edmund Arrowsmith Catholic High School, Ashton-in-Makerfield

I Dreamed A Dream

The icy wind blows ferociously against my cheek,
Great gasps of air getting blown and tossed
I look around, too scared to speak
Because I am completely, hopelessly lost

At the tip of the mountain, feet covered with snow
My face is wet and begins to glow
I peer over the mountain, trying to find help
And I stumble and with a huge yelp
I fall down,
        Down,
            Thud!

I'm in an icy cold lake, teeth chattering with cold
But over there is a huge pile of gold!
I swim to my fate, but as soon as I try,
I go under and under . . . 'Help!' I cry
I'm sinking and sinking, I'm going to die!

Moments later I wake up with a scream
For I have just dreamed the most terrible dream.

Sarah Parkinson (12)
St Edmund Arrowsmith Catholic High School, Ashton-in-Makerfield

I Dreamed A Dream!

I'm on the swing,
At the park,
The fun ends
And the scariness starts.

Pondering round,
In the soft golden sand,
I fall through my swing
And on metal I land.

I quickly stand,
A sound I hear,
A giant robot,
Is getting near.

Running and running,
But no escape,
This maze-like path,
Is my fate.

I can see the end,
I've just got to run,
The robot's still here,
This is no fun.

I reach the middle,
I reach my goal,
I'm at the park,
Where the swing lay stone cold.

Amy Cotton (11)
St Edmund Arrowsmith Catholic High School, Ashton-in-Makerfield

Untitled

I have a dream that no one can see,
My mind, my thoughts and my feelings are everywhere.

I have a dream that only I can see,
Inside my head only I have the key.

I have a dream that only I know what's going on,
Inside the locked box of my mind.

I have a dream that no one can hear,
In my mind there's no one near.

I have a dream that doesn't seem to end,
I just keep getting to another bend.

I have a dream, a dream that I am sliding down a rainbow,
All the different colours go over my head in stripes
And I come to a door so I open it and walk in
And I am back in my bedroom
And I realise that it was all a dream.

Charlotte Mayes (12)
St Edmund Arrowsmith Catholic High School, Ashton-in-Makerfield

I Have A Dream

I have a dream that when I'm old,
I will e confident and bold.
That catwalk is where I want to be,
Modelling clothes for all to see.

I would talk to people, I'm not shy,
I'm not the girl who would sit and cry
Because she thought the insults were true,
But now her beauty shines right through.

My dream for the world is that all girls will
Feel as beautiful as they should.

Nicola Curry (12)
Trinity School, Carlisle

I Have A Dream

I have a dream that the world will make peace.
The wars and the heartbreak will all decrease.

If we don't stop then all we will hear is the bang.
The silence, the end of the world.

I have a dream that pollution will stop
And all of our weapons we will soon drop.

If we don't stop then all we will hear is the bang,
The silence, the end of the world.

I have a dream we will stop grabbing money
And we will sit and listen to the bees making honey.

If we don't stop then all we will hear is the bang,
The silence, the end of the world.

I have a dream we will stop being vicious
And spreading lies which are untrue and malicious.

If we don't stop then all we will hear is the bang,
The silence, the end of the world.

Think about these words and stop your evil ways,
Or all you will hear is the bang, the silence, the end of the world.

Lucy Meekley (12)
Trinity School, Carlisle

I Have A Dream

I have a dream, not just any dream.
A dream of peace and love,
A dream of eternal life.

I have a dream where the world's green and healthy.
A place of life and happiness.
I have a dream of a safe and secure world,

A perfect world!

Jack Mallam (12)
Trinity School, Carlisle

Imagine!

I can see the world as a better place,
I can imagine the gentle sea with no economic waste,
I can see the streets clear of rubbish,
I can imagine gum-free floors all over the place,
I can see the walls graffiti-free,
I can imagine the young voices gentle and fresh.

You can dream the world is a better place,
You can look at a happy child's face,
You can dream of a bully-free workplace,
You can look at equality in every space,
You can dream of a peaceful living space,
You can look at a future united as one.

We can observe the world as a better place,
We can view the world racist-free to black and white.
We can observe no smog or grey in our sky,
We can view the roads empty of lorries and cars,
We can observe petrol stations bare and sparse,
We can view buses jam-packed and see the stars.

Hannah Edwards (13)
Trinity School, Carlisle

I Have A Dream

I have a dream,
A dream to stop all whips,
To stop all whips that hit,
Whips that hit those poor horses,
Those poor race horses,
Those races that are cruel,
They have to run and run,
With jockeys that hit,
When they run over the finish line in first place,
With no trace of praise,
Those poor, poor horses.

Zoe Blythe (12)
Trinity School, Carlisle

I Have A Dream

I have a dream that there are no more wars
Or animals in the world,
So that no more people get killed or hurt.
So that there are no more people that have to mourn
Over all the evil people who did bad things
To relatives or the family of certain people.

I have a dream that when I'm older
I will become a world famous football player
And play in the Premiership for Manchester United
And win the league title.
Overall I want to be the best player in the world
And be captain of a World Cup winning team.

Brandon Longcake (11)
Trinity School, Carlisle

A Dream . . .

Once upon a time lived a dream,
A dream that will change the world,
Make us a team.
All wars will be stopped,
All weapons will be dropped.
Cruelty to animals is wrong,
All those animals are scared all day long.
That people will not fight,
Whether they are black or white.
Poverty is not fair,
We have loads of food, so share.
A dream once lived
And forever it will last.

Rebecca Dixon (12)
Trinity School, Carlisle

I Have A Dream . . .

A world where no one is killed
where people won't sit and cry
no one is better than anyone else
and people are accepted for who they are

If leaders could change things easily
no wars or starvation
everyone can have their say
bullies just get out of the way.

A world where no one is scared
to achieve anything they want to
no one will stand in their way
I have a dream like that

I want to be successful
in everything I do.
So many places I want to see
so many faces I want to meet
so many things I want to be
but no one is saying in any way
that my dream will not come true!

Abbie Brayton (12)
Trinity School, Carlisle

I Dream . . .

I dream that the world will be
Nice and peaceful, calm and free

The animals and flower beds,
At night they all will rest their heads.

The stars will twinkle, moon shines bright,
Waiting till the morning light.

Andi Menzies (12)
Trinity School, Carlisle

I Have A Dream!

I have a dream that one day love and peace
will be the main aim for most people in life.

This is what everyone should want!

Everyone in their right mind will stop dropping litter
and find a bin to put it in instead.

I have a dream that all these wars will stop
and people will go home to their families
so that the heartache will stop as well.

This is what everyone should want!

I have a dream that pollution will stop
and people will understand why.

This is what everyone should want!

I have a dream that in the future
no one will know what a weapon is.

This is what everyone should want!

Remember these words or else all there will be
is silence and blackness!

Dominique Toms (12)
Trinity School, Carlisle

Messy World

M e, you, us, all of us.
E verything in the world is a mess
S o do something about it, there is
S omething you can do.
Y ou can do something too.

W hy is it such a mess?
O ur world, we are responsible
R unning round, tidy up
L ove our world
D on't drop it, *stop it!*

Trudi Newgarth (11)
Trinity School, Carlisle

My Dream

My dream is to play for LFC or even CUFC,
To wear the number seven shirt and win the Champions League,
I'll play until I'm fifty-five and score three hundred goals.
I'll score three hundred wonder goals and win the Premiership,
When I retire I'll manage Liverpool and have my statue built.

My dream for the world is to stop all racism and all poverty.
People who are racist will have to go to prison
And big homes will be built for the homeless all over the world.

Ben Bolton (12)
Trinity School, Carlisle

The World's Dream

T he world's dream would be . . .
H elping others in difficult times
E very day trying to solve each other's problems

W hile everyone is nice and kind
O thers lend a helping hand
R esolve problems that need solving
L oving, calm and peaceful world
D ifferent people talking soothingly
S ometimes when we're all feeling down
　　someone shouts, 'Please don't frown.'

D ilemma we're all in, no one says a nasty word
R edeemed is the world
E veryone is happy as Larry
A nd everyone is . . .
M errily chatting.

Alex Armstrong (11)
Trinity School, Carlisle

I Have A Dream

I have a dream, that one day
I will become a model and be famous
Have the latest fashion items
And wear them for all to see
Cat-walking down the stage
Is where I want to be
Glam and glitter modelling clothes
Pretty and bonny for all my shows
I have a dream for the world
That all wars will end
And peace will be brought to the world.

Samantha Barker (12)
Trinity School, Carlisle

My Dream

My dream is to be a professional football player
And play in the World Cup for England
But first I want to play for my local team
That has been my lifetime ambition.

Liam Gilmour (12)
Trinity School, Carlisle

Imagine

I magine a perfect world
M oney is not a problem anymore
A world without racism
G oodness is in everyone's heart
I can imagine this world
N astiness is in the past
E veryone is loved.

Ashley Fortis (14)
Walbottle Campus Technology College, Walbottle

I Have A Dream

I have a dream

H elping the poor
A nd stopping racism
V ery healthy people all around the world, so
E veryone can be themselves

A nimals can go free

D octors and nurses can go to Third World countries
R ights are for everyone
E veryone is equal
A nyone can help the world
M oney is not a problem anymore.

Danielle Robson (14)
Walbottle Campus Technology College, Walbottle

Climate Change

C oldness turns to warmth
L ife will be destroyed
I ce caps will melt
M any people's lives will change
A nimals will become extinct
T error will hit the world
E verybody will be miserable

C ooked, the Earth will be
H eatwaves will come
A dventurers will not go on exhibitions
N othing but rising sea levels
G reenhouse gases destroy the ozone layer
E arth will be a disaster.

Sean McMahon-Harris (13)
Walbottle Campus Technology College, Walbottle

I Have A Dream

I have a dream, or a wish you could call it,
The sight of the world in the eyes of a hornet.
Just imagine the sight of the world in other's eyes,
Try your best, you'll be surprised.
The poverty in the nation and all the racism.
The people with no money
And the people that bully.
The wars in the world all still hold grudges,
Even though it's ended now people are the judges.
It's hard to think of a world at peace,
Unless we work together and release.

That was my dream beginning to end
Don't let the world come to an end.

Jayde Kennedy (14)
Walbottle Campus Technology College, Walbottle

Imagine

Imagine if everyone was totally rich,
Imagine if racism could just be ditched.

Imagine if life was peaceful and calm,
Imagine if nobody came to harm.

Imagine if children were pleasant and kind,
Imagine if we could just simply unwind.

Imagine a stress-free world for us all,
Imagine if the media couldn't buy our soul.

Imagine if everyone got on with each other,
Imagine all the offspring, one after the other.

Imagine if everybody was totally free,
You've been imagining a world just like me!

Sophie Mansuy (13)
Walbottle Campus Technology College, Walbottle

I Have A Dream

I have a dream
Of a big quiet world,
Where children have fun,
Where there is no need for a nun,
A world where every child is loved by a mum,
A world when you're not alone,
Will my dream come true?

A world I used to have
Every child has a smile,
Every man has some clothes,
Every stomach stuffed full,
Every woman with a husband,
Every man with a wife,
Every child, with love all around him,
But that is now gone.

A world we need
The crops grow tall,
The trees are numerous,
All animals in a family,
A world with no need for a hospital,
Every house fit for a king,
Every child, with an educated brain,
That's all we need.

A world today,
A child all alone,
Searching for a home,
Then let down when he finds love
And when looking around,
He only found
More prisons than schools,
More orphans than pupils,
More families split up every day,
This is the world today.

A world we will never have,
A big quiet world,
Where children have fun,
A world where there is no need for a nun,
A world where every child is loved by a mum,
A world where no one is alone,
Will our dreams ever come true?

Hopefully yes, but for now it seems no,
Look at all these children, woe, woe, woe.

Jamie Foggo (13)
Walbottle Campus Technology College, Walbottle

I Have A Dream . . .

I have a dream
M ore rights
A lot of freedom
G ood people
I have a dream of a new world
N o racism
E qual rights

A dream of a

N ew world
E ngland
W ith the rest of the world

W orried
O dds against
R ights
L ong term
D iscussion

R acism gone
I have a wish of no climate changes
G oing on about rights
H ave important rights
T olerance gone
S oul of people gone.

Carl Gilchrist (14)
Walbottle Campus Technology College, Walbottle

I Have A Dream

I have a dream of peace and love
Of a world where war is a thing of the past
Where friendship is as true as a dove
This is my world of peace and love

I have a dream where poverty is gone
Of a world where we are equal as one
Where money is worthless
And love escapes none
This is my world where poverty is gone

I have a dream where rules are followed
Where there is no crime
Where no trees are hollowed
This is my world where rules are followed

I have a dream where the world is cared for
Where no one asks for more
Where hate is at an all-time low
This is my world that is cared for

I have a dream of a world with no bullies
Where life is made of simple decisions
Where people like to help and care
This is my world with no bullies

I have a dream of no puppy farms
And dogs are safe from harm
Where animal abuse never exists
This is my world with no puppy farms.

I have a dream where everything's fair
And you don't get bullied for the style of your hair
And matches can end in a draw
This is my world where everything's fair

I have a dream of a world without adults
And criminals no more
And where children have a say
This is my world without adults

This is why I dream.

Christopher Burn (13)
Walbottle Campus Technology College, Walbottle

I Have A Dream

I have a dream,
Where dark shadows are filled with light,
Where black and white walk hand in hand,
Where wrongs are put right.

I have a dream,
Where no one lives in fear,
Where worries are overcome,
Where laws are obeyed.

I have a dream,
Where money doesn't matter,
Where poverty is a thing of the past,
Where animals are free to roam.

I have a dream,
Where happiness is the most important emotion,
Where friendship is essential,
Where love is the fulfilled feeling.

I have a dream,
Where the elderly are respected,
Where people are happy to be who they are,
Where children feel safe.

I have a dream,
Where war has no purpose,
Where all the citizens of the world are equal,
Where all the countries support each other.

I have a dream,
Where everyone is accepted for who they are,
Where both women and men are united,
Where dreams are a reality.

I have a dream,
Where the world never ends,
Where everyone can look forward to their future,
Because their future is bright and full of hope.

This is my dream.

Kayleigh Lambert (13)
Walbottle Campus Technology College, Walbottle

I Have A Dream . . .

Where friendship is everything
And labels mean nothing
Where love is all that matters
And hate means nothing at all

Where nature is still beautiful
And smiles are contagious
Where a bumblebee is valued
And laughter is heard above everything else

Where animals run free from captivity
And birds pattern the sky
Where fur coats are forgotten
And the countryside is as peaceful as a sleeping baby

Where hoof beats are for heartbeats
And everyone has friends like I do
And no one is afraid to dream
Where dreams are a reality

I have a dream . . .

Michelle Hunter (13)
Walbottle Campus Technology College, Walbottle

I Have A Dream

I have a dream!
I have a dream of no bullying,
I have a dream of no loneliness,
I have a dream of no hate,
I have a dream that everyone is treated equally,
I have a dream that people will stop the abuse.
I have a dream!

Rebecca Pearson (13)
Walbottle Campus Technology College, Walbottle

A Perfect World

I have a dream where this world, is my world,
A perfect world, where animals and plants can live freely,
Where no more forests are turned into your furniture,
A world where no one suffers.

In my world the sun would always shine
And the birds would always sing,
Where every life is valued from tall tree to small ant,
Where fish can swim in clean fresh waters,
Instead of infected and poisonous acids.

Where we sheathe our swords and lower our bows,
Because there is no enemy, only friends,
Where destruction is despised and peace honoured,
The end of fighting, and the start, the real start,
Of global friendship.

A world where colour doesn't matter and everyone is equal,
The mountains, rivers and forests are left to grow freely,
To be left for the animals to reinhabit what they long ago vacated,
Due to the cruelty and evil of the past world . . .

Peter Watson (13)
Walbottle Campus Technology College, Walbottle

I Have A Dream

I have a dream of a faraway beach
Perfect, a paradise, almost out of reach
Soft grains of sand, pure and white
The sun, so golden, it blinds your sight
Crystal-blue water and big green palm trees
A shade from the sunlight, swaying gently in the breeze
A campfire burning in the middle of the night
Smiling and happiness, as the stars shine bright
Perfect, a paradise, almost out of reach
I have a dream of a faraway beach.

Beth Atkin (12)
Walbottle Campus Technology College, Walbottle

When I Dream

The world is united,
Together like a team,
Disasters never occur
And everyone has their say.

Flowers blossom in winter,
There is no such thing as a miserable day,
Everyone wins competitions like these
And the sky is always blue.

Soldiers survive,
War is a thing of the past,
Young children don't die every day
And poverty is no more.

This is my perfect world in my dreams,
Where everyone is in peace.

Hollie Slack (13)
Walbottle Campus Technology College, Walbottle

I Have A Dream

I dream of a world full of love.

H atred is an unknown word.
A world where there is no crime.
V iolence is never the answer.
E verybody is at peace with one another.

A world where no one fights or bullies.

D reams aren't impossible.
R eally, they do come true.
E veryone is equal.
A nd that means me and you!
M y world would be the perfect world.

Sam Kingham (13)
Walbottle Campus Technology College, Walbottle

I Have A Dream

I have a dream,
Where tobacco doesn't have a place in people's lungs,
Where people aren't reduced to tears by bullies,
Where a smile doesn't need to be infectious,
Where animals are treated with respect,
Where poverty is extinct and first, second and third class
Is non-existent.

I have a dream of a world
Where our climate is unchanged,
Where love is blooming everywhere,
Where war is never the answer,
Where friendship comes in small doses but means a lot,
Where nobody is judged by the way they look.

I have a dream.

Kirsty Forster (13)
Walbottle Campus Technology College, Walbottle

My Dream The Other Night

I had a dream the other night where friends were forever,
Where friends knew everything about each other,
Where friends can always be bothered.

My dream reminded me of something,
It played on my mind,
What was that something?

Then I remembered what it was,
My dream was actually reality,
My friends are forever
And we know everything about each other.

My friends are the best ever
And we will stay friends forever!

Amy Lawson (13)
Walbottle Campus Technology College, Walbottle

I Have A Dream

I have a dream

A world with no racism
Where skin colour doesn't matter
And designer labels make no difference
So then no one gets put down

Where poverty is unknown
So everyone runs round full
Where climate change doesn't exist
So the world will not end

Where adults aren't so bossy
And police don't exist
So children can wander the streets
Without getting funny looks

A world with no bullying
Where kicking and punching is unseen
Where people don't trip each other
And everything is calm

I have a dream.

Louise Forster (13)
Walbottle Campus Technology College, Walbottle

My Dream

I have a dream where the skies are always blue
Everyone has a dream and this is mine

A dream where poverty comes to an end
Where the rivers flow free
Where global warming is nothing
Where everyone gets along

I made a promise to obey the laws
And other people should too
Everyone has a dream and this is mine
To make the world a better place.

Katie Makepeace (13)
Walbottle Campus Technology College, Walbottle

I Have A Dream . . .

You walk into the room,
Run your hands through my hair,
You raise me by the hips
And hold me there.

You turn on the music
And start moving to the beat,
We glide across the room,
By the balls of our feet.

Cos when I'm with you,
The music really matters,
The reflection of my eyes,
My lips, you start to flatter.

The lights come back on,
The music starts to end,
You let go and walk away,
Telling me I'm just a friend.

I have a dream . . .

Rachael Mowat (13)
Walbottle Campus Technology College, Walbottle

If

If the world had peace not war,
The sky were blue not black,
If there was more nature than factories,
If we could all recycle what we could,
No litter on the streets,
Just happiness and good looks, like in little pleats
If there was no violence, no bullying,
Just enjoyment throughout the world,
Then there wouldn't be a fight,
Just beautiful strong light,
We can get this world right,
With all of our power and might.

Ross Tweedy (13)
Walbottle Campus Technology College, Walbottle

I Have A Dream

No police and the world will run wild
Then people will have a lot of money
We will have more happiness without them
No longer will poverty rule our world
We will have more friends
No one will starve
No more racism
Then that will be my perfect world

We can live happily together
No more will we fight
Then we can all be friends
We will be kind to each other
No one will bully
Then people will listen
We will really like it
No one will regret that

Then our world will be great
We will not fear war
No one needs to be scared
Then war will stop indefinitely
We will love that order
No one will disagree
Then it will be great
We love it

No one will fight
Then our world will be peaceful
We will be great as a team
No one will hate that
Then our world will be great
We are super
No one will regret that
Then we love it.

James Bennett (13)
Walbottle Campus Technology College, Walbottle

I Have A Dream

I have a dream the world will be one
Terrorism and war, there will be none.
No car bombs, no attacks
No bombs in the air or bombs on train tracks.

I wish we would all change!

No tramps on the street with their dirty feet
No rich countries, more soup kitchens too
No rummaging through bags,
It's all up to you.

I wish we would all change!

No diseases that kill
I wish we could take a simple pill
No viruses around
No death or syringes on the ground.

I wish we would all change!

No pollution in rivers
That gives me the shivers
No contaminating a pond,
Why can't we wave a wand?

No polluting the streams
These are my dreams
They could come true . . .

. . . it's up to you!

Craig Baines (13)
Walbottle Campus Technology College, Walbottle

I Have A Dream

I have a dream
For everyone to have a friend,
To have someone who likes you for you,
So you never have to pretend.

To have someone to tell your secrets to
And who will always listen to you.
Even when problems occur
And worst comes to worst,
This person will always put you first.

So I'll spread my wings
And learn to fly
And send these notes up to the sky
And maybe one day,
They will reach the top
And everyone will have a friend
And loneliness will stop.

Georgia Dodds (13)
Walbottle Campus Technology College, Walbottle

Untitled

The world with peace would be fun,
Fighting, stabbing, shooting guns,
When coming out late at night,
People get a horrible fight.

Mugging, grabbing, fighting and stabbing,
Blood all over, on the floor,
Waking up very sore.
All happens on a night out,
All you want to do is shout,
Gangsters, the Mafia dealing with guns,
This world with peace would be fun.

Danny Bowers (13)
Walbottle Campus Technology College, Walbottle

I Have A Dream

A nimals are respected as feeling like humans

P eople have smiles on their faces
E verybody is able to roam freely
R acism never existed
F airness is normal
E qual opportunities, whoever you are
C olour doesn't matter
T here is no such thing as 'war'

W eapons have no reason
O ther religions are accepted
R eality is like a fantasy
L eopards aren't killed for their skin
D reams come true.

Amy Rebair (13)
Walbottle Campus Technology College, Walbottle

I Hate War

I have a dream
And in my dream
I imagine a world
Where there is no war,
No one is killed,
There's no such thing as a bully,
There's no such thing as tobacco.
No one is classed
Any higher or lower than anyone else.
No animal is bruised
And no person is hit.
I have a dream
That all is fair.

Kelly Briggs (13)
Walbottle Campus Technology College, Walbottle

I Have A Dream . . .

I have a dream . . .
Where poverty is made history,
Where starving people don't search for food,
Where everyone is sheltered,
My dream will come true.

I have a dream . . .
Where happiness is not a crime,
Where everyone can get along,
Where everyone always smiles,
My dream will come true.

I have a dream . . .
Where animals can be treated like humans,
Where animals have a right to live,
Where animal testing is illegal,
My dream will come true.

I have a dream . . .
That all my dreams can come true,
That one day everyone can live freely,
That happiness and peace isn't a crime,
If my dreams come true, the world would be perfect.

Bhavini Shukla (13)
Walbottle Campus Technology College, Walbottle

I Have A Dream

I have a dream where animals roam the land.
I have a dream where zoos let them free.
I have a dream where puppy farms are banned.
I have a dream where test labs close.

I have a dream where goths and chavs get on fine.
I have a dream where there is a better democracy.
I have a dream that everyone has a home to go to at night.
But most of all I dream that everyone is free.

Stacey Shoker (13)
Walbottle Campus Technology College, Walbottle

I Have A Dream

What if the world were happy?
What if there was no more sadness?
What if the world were peaceful?
What if there was no more war?
What if there was no more hate?
What if everyone got along?

What if there was no more poverty
To make starving children happy?
What if there was no more bullying
To stop children hiding in fear?
What if the world was perfect
To make everybody happy?

Michael Dobson (13)
Walbottle Campus Technology College, Walbottle

I Have A Dream

I have a dream
I'm a star in the sky
I have a dream
I can learn to fly
I have a dream
I am free
I have a dream
I can swim in the sea
I have a dream
Everyone has a friend like mine
I have a dream
Everything is fine

But most of all I'd like to say
I have a dream the world is OK!

Sarah Bambrough (13)
Walbottle Campus Technology College, Walbottle

I Have A Dream . . .

Think of a world where no one is hungry.
Think of a world where everyone is healthy.
Think of a world with food and water for everyone.
I have a dream, where poverty doesn't exist.

Think of a world with no black or white.
Think of a world with no line of division.
Think of a world where all cultures think as one.
I have a dream, where racism doesn't exist.

Think of a world where we all get along.
Think of a world where nobody feels rejected.
Think of a world where cruelty is abandoned.
I have a dream, where bullies don't exist.

I have a dream, *we* can change the world.

Paige Temperley (13)
Walbottle Campus Technology College, Walbottle

What Is A Dream?

What is a dream?

A figment of our imagination
A stretch of the mind
Where racism and poverty stop

We always say but never do
We always want but never get

No I don't have a dream, I have a goal
A goal to make a sanctuary
Where equality is the only thing that matters
Where starvation doesn't exist

My goal will wipe out all suffering and hate
The term 'living the dream' will finally be recognised

But, what is good when there is no hate?

Rosul Mokhtar (13)
Walbottle Campus Technology College, Walbottle

I Have A Dream

I dream that some day tyrants will not rule the world
And all things will be united under one banner.
All shall live among another in times of peace, not war.
So that there will be no racism or discrimination.

I wish that no person should have to suffer,
That all people should have food, water and shelter
And no one should die or suffer from diseases
Or lose their parents or a loved one.

I hope that the world will not be destroyed by pollution
And that it will be a clean and safe environment for our children,
So that animal habitats will not be destroyed
And trees will not be cut down for fuel.

I pray that one day there will be no wars or fighting
And every person has the same religion so no one can argue
or disagree.
All humans should work together to solve problems,
That all the chaos in the world today will vanish and there
will be peace.

I have a dream . . .

Matthew Summers (13)
Walbottle Campus Technology College, Walbottle

In My Dream

In my dream I wish I could fly,
So I could watch the world from way up high.

I want to explore the sky,
And be unable to die.

For everyone to live forever,
And everyone to join together.

To make my dream come true.

Chris Shorter (14)
Walbottle Campus Technology College, Walbottle

I Have A Dream

I have a dream that the world is a peaceful and happy place

That every living person has a family and a house to go to
and someone to love them

I dream that cancer is destroyed and doesn't destroy
so many people's lives

That the word war has ended
and never will return

I wish that factories were knocked down
so there was no pollution

Racism is unfair to those who really matter

The world may never be a wonderful peaceful place
but *please* let's try!

Rebecca Foster (13)
Walbottle Campus Technology College, Walbottle

Imagine

Imagine standing with no grass under you,
Imagine there is nothing you can do.
Imagine no animals, no birds, no bees,
Imagine no money or even fees.
Imagine a place with no love, no one happy,
Imagine no food, restaurants or café.
Imagine no shelter to sleep under at night,
Imagine no colours, red, blue or white.
Imagine having no husband or wife,
Imagine this will be some people's life.

Stephanie Guy (13)
Walbottle Campus Technology College, Walbottle

I Have A Dream

I have a dream:
> where the world can live in peace,
> and where we put poverty to an end,
> where racism is shown the red card,
> where all homeless people have a bed.

I have a dream:
> where black and white people are treated equally,
> where we treat everyone with respect,
> where different is good,
> where animals are loved and live freely.

I have a dream:
> where war is never spoken of,
> and crime doesn't exist,
> where men and women roam freely,
> that's my perfect world.

Jonathon Bartlett (13)
Walbottle Campus Technology College, Walbottle

I Wish For A World

I wish for a world
Of land and sea
Where we can jump
From wake to wake
We land smooth
Go back over the wake
To do one handers
Then state:

'I wish the world was full of care
No homeless person in this world
No disease, no wars
Just happiness and
Everything running smooth
Just like the wakeboard.'

Aaron Clasper (13)
Walbottle Campus Technology College, Walbottle

I Have A Dream

I dream for a world . . .
Where peace brings the world together
Where we can stop bullying once and for all
Where all the homeless children can be loved and cherished
With a full stomach
Where hope brings love and humanity.

I wish for a world . . .
Where the moon and the stars shine bright at night
Where doctors can cure illnesses with a click of their fingers
Where people are unique in their own way
Where racism makes people equal

I hope for a world . . .
Where war has come to an end
Where birds can fly high above the treetops
Where the rich can help the poor
Where guns are banned for good

I pray for a world . . .
Where friendship brings happy faces
Where the answer is not revenge
Where everyone can join in on the games
And where people can see through the eyes of another

In my world . . .
Our eyes are placed in front because
It's easier to look forward than behind.

Holly Laws (14)
Walbottle Campus Technology College, Walbottle

I Have A Dream

I have a dream

Where everyone will just get along
No fighting, no war and no more poverty
Where everyone has clean water
Fresh food, fresh water, fresh air
We should all spread our riches

We should all listen to one another
And stand up for what we believe in
People should be bullied by no one
We should cut down on pollution
We should all distribute our wealth

I have a dream

To make sure that all countries have foundations to live
Where everyone has a say
We should live in a world where children come first
Where crime is ended
And terrorism is a distant memory
Where it ain't just all big names
Where we all respect one another

I have a dream

Where everyone has a purpose
Where no one criticises one another
Where we all have dreams
Where you can become what you want
We all have a dream.

Jake Richardson (13)
Walbottle Campus Technology College, Walbottle

I Have A Dream

My dream is not about changing the environment,
changing one place, it's about changing a nation.
My dream is a place where nobody is treated differently
because of their skin colour.
Not a place where there are two worlds
and the price of admission to our world is white skin.
My dream is just a vision, but in time, it will become a reality.

My dream asks little of the world,
it asks for a place where nobody is showered with technology,
giving them happiness, while others are slaves to the others,
upper class communities.
In my dream, there are no upper, middle and lower classes.
Everybody lives equally and that way, the world is a place
of no jealousy and hate and that the world is free of worry.

My dream is a place where children can roam the streets
with people of their choice,
not worried about being a bad influence on them,
not worried about coming home embedded in cuts or stab wounds,
not worried about what dangers their eyes may be exposed to.
My dream is about change and a change of environment is what
is needed to make the world better.

Finally, my dream concludes with the world pulling together,
everybody living together, people, creatures, plants, race, place,
gender, don't matter in my world, because you are always recognised,
wherever you are.

Daniel Gilbert (13)
Walbottle Campus Technology College, Walbottle

I Have A Dream

Can you imagine a world where we all live in peace and harmony,
where we live together with all creatures and even with each other,
where the world is united as one?

A world where war has been destroyed,
fear has been scared away and
where the darkness is too dark to see.
Where poverty has died of hunger
and where disease has infected itself.

A world where children can play in happiness
and not play in fear.
Fear of what lies outside their door.
An unknown world for most people,
a world they may never understand
as there is too much violence and fear to follow.

A place where the stars and the moon shine bright
and where the sun shines brighter.
Where every voice is heard and every opinion is thought about,
where difference is a good thing, not a good thing for bullies.

A place where technology doesn't rule our lives
and where we have the right to do as we wish.
A place where we still roam around the world
searching for new adventures.

I can imagine a world where we all live in peace and harmony,
where we live together with all creatures, even with each other,
where the whole world is united as one.
Let's build this world together, as one.

Connor M Roberts (13)
Walbottle Campus Technology College, Walbottle

Please!

I have a dream that one day in this world
people won't hurt little boys and girls.

People walk around with guns and grenades
there are all sorts of diseases
like cancer and AIDS.

I have a dream that one day in this world
people will be loving and caring
not horrible and daring.

There are people sitting on the streets
just please give them some treats.

I have a dream that one day in this world
pollution will stop, you're killing us

Please do not!

Amy Thompson (14)
Walbottle Campus Technology College, Walbottle

I Have A Dream!

Where poverty isn't a word,
Where nobody is scared,
Where racism doesn't exist.

Where discrimination doesn't hurt
Where children can have a life of fun
And childhood memories are full of joy.
Where every illness has a cure.

I wish every man had justice
Man-made disasters were deceased
Every person had privileges

I have a dream.

Megan Armstrong (13)
Walbottle Campus Technology College, Walbottle

About The World!

I had a dream
A kind of a scheme
To make this world a better place
For you and me
To save the human race.

I had a dream
A kind of a scheme
Drugs, fighting, crime and war
That's what you and me don't ask for.

I had a dream
That wars will end
And peace will reign
So people will gain
The freedom to heal our world.

I have a dream
To live with the free
No disease, no hunger, no thirst
We are all equal in our world
Behold my words and heed my dream.

Emma Larrad (14)
Walbottle Campus Technology College, Walbottle

I Have A Dream!

I have a dream
that school doesn't exist,
kids play in the sun
and rain isn't missed.
Happiness is there
and hatred nowhere.
The rich and the poor
together as one.
The liars and the fighting
all of a sudden, gone!

Sheryl Munroe (14)
Walbottle Campus Technology College, Walbottle

I Dream It Will End . . .

I get off the school bus and start to walk home,
It's a long walk, it's scary, I am all alone.
I cross at the traffic lights because Mum said I should,
When I get over they're waiting, wearing hoods.
My heart begins to race,
My feet moving at a quicker pace.
I try to turn around and see where they are,
I can sense they're near but aren't too far.
I know what's coming, they can sense my fear,
I listen to them calling, 'Come over here!'
I'm full of hatred and dread,
For what is coming ahead.
I don't know why I turn around,
I can see the look on their faces . . .
I don't make a sound.

Rachel Dickinson (14)
Walbottle Campus Technology College, Walbottle

I Have A Dream

I have a dream
that school doesn't exist
children play in the sun
not in the mist.
The delight is released
and the terror deceased.
The rich and the poor
united as one.
No wars being fought
no shooting or bombs.
Countries together
with love and no hate.
The world at the moment
is ever so great.

Jack Routledge (14)
Walbottle Campus Technology College, Walbottle

I Have A Dream

I dream of a world
A perfect world
Happiness and world peace
A world where everyone is equal
Where sadness, hunger and war never existed.

A world where it's summer all year round
Where winter has not yet been discovered
The bitterness, cold, darkness . . . are extinct.

A world where all humans are treated the same
A world where everyone is rich
Where everyone is famous
Because when everyone is rich and famous
No one will be.

Kerry Donnelly (13)
Walbottle Campus Technology College, Walbottle

I Have A Dream

My team is the best
They will always beat the rest.
Chelsea this, us next
With Owen up front
And Parker in the middle.
I do have a dream
The title is ours
We will celebrate in bars
I do have a dream
My team is the Toon
My team will never go doon
My dream, *Newcastle*.

Chris Simmons (14)
Walbottle Campus Technology College, Walbottle

I Have A Dream

I have a dream
that there will be no war.
I have a dream
to stop terrorism and bombing
because innocent children are dying.
I have a dream
to have more money
to help developing countries.

I have a dream
to have lots of money
to give to the homeless people
because they are starving and feeling cold.
I have a dream
there will be no shooting, raping and kidnapping.

I have a dream
to make myself a better person.
I've realised all the horrible things
in the world are nasty.

Agatha Kona (13)
Walbottle Campus Technology College, Walbottle

I Have A Dream - Haikus

Sunset below us,
Dark shadows stay by my feet,
I dream of world peace.

Dark black and blue marks,
Long winding path of violence,
I dream of world peace.

Samantha Turner
Walbottle Campus Technology College, Walbottle

I Have A Dream

I have a dream of no wars.
I dream to step through a peace door.
I dream weapons are banned.
I dream people aren't disrespected
Because they are tanned.

I have a dream of no child abuse.
I dream all killings will reduce.
I dream of no animal testing.
I dream dead people are just resting.

I have a dream there are no strikes.
I dream everyone has their dream bike.
I dream that everyone has love.
I dream it all comes with a white dove.

Charlotte Fisher
Walbottle Campus Technology College, Walbottle

I Have A Dream

I have a dream
nightfall arrives,
alleyway of steam
whispered lives.

Dusk becomes bare,
day develops night,
mist pours into air,
sets off my sight.

Distant screams,
murmured cries,
terrified dreams,
come alive.

Andrew Walker (13)
Walbottle Campus Technology College, Walbottle

Dream For peace

Dream.
Why should we need to dream for peace,
We should see it every day
Where guns are gone and the fighting's ceased.

Why?
Why haven't we learned from past mistakes?
Wars that have shook the foundations of this very Earth
Where men, women and children's lives are at stake.

Pain.
Why do we feel this pain?
The grief tears us limb from limb
We shouldn't lose, but gain.

Sorrow.
Families' lives torn by sorrow,
The loss of a child, their only one
They can only wish for a better tomorrow.

Hope.
One day our dreams of hope will come true,
Families, towns, nations recovered
Where discrimination is lost too.

I wish, hope, dream and pray that
The world will be at peace some day.

Amy Vaughan (14)
Walbottle Campus Technology College, Walbottle

I Have A Dream

I have a dream
That one day we will live in peace
And harmony,
Where no weapons are needed
And no men need die
For the sake of others
And the people that control them.

No reason is good enough
For people who are in high places,
To order others
To their death,
To fight a battle
That they should be fighting themselves.

Either in a muddy field
Or a high-tech base,
Bombs and pistols, guns and knives
They all cause bloodshed
And unearthly pain
For the ones they catch
In their web.

Clare Goodwin (13)
Walbottle Campus Technology College, Walbottle

Help This Dream!

In the future I hope that everyone is free,
that will achieve for you and me,
even though that is a dream
we can work together in a team.
Altogether we can help mankind
to ease each other and unwind
and to get rid of stress.
Whether you wear trousers or a dress,
to cheer up each other day by day,
we can help each other on our way,
make each other be heard,
to not be offended by a single word,
to make this dream come true,
to help each other to not say, 'Who?'
But to know each other in a way
that you can trust them day after day.
Remember this, do not stereotype,
it is wrong, it is not right.

Claire Packham (14)
Walbottle Campus Technology College, Walbottle

I Dream

I dream for a world where no wars take place.
I dream for a world where all diseases are cured.
I dream for a world where all bullying has a full stop.

I wish for a world when nobody is poor.
I wish for a world where everybody is happy.
I wish for a world where everything is fair.
I wish for a world where everybody has money.

Peter Ward (14)
Walbottle Campus Technology College, Walbottle

I Have A Dream

When one life ends, another begins
A pure life without any sins
If only everything could be like that.

I have a dream for love and peace
And all the war and crimes to cease
Everyone's like each other.

But how
How can we ever continue to exist like this?

In this uncivilised world of war
No one thinks of what others saw.
Those poor, poor people caught up in it all.

Traumatising lives lie ahead
For those few children lying down to bed.

I have a dream.

Gabriella Michelini (14)
Walbottle Campus Technology College, Walbottle

I Have A Dream

I have a dream where abuse is unknown,
Where pain is replaced by laughter and love.
I have a dream where the fighting has ended
And where war is just a myth.
I have a dream where thousands are born
Born to better lives.
I have a dream that this is not a dream,
But everybody's perfect world.

Rebecca Goodall (14)
Walbottle Campus Technology College, Walbottle

I Have A Dream

Why is the world full of bullies?
Why can't we all live in peace?
There are always problems and rivalries,
Everywhere we go, we witness it.
It's all down to thinking you're better!

Tick-tock, time goes by.
Problems getting better or worse?
Racism, poverty, terrorism just a few,
Scaring, shock, stop this now!
It's all down to thinking you're better!

People put in poverty,
Less food, less water, badly paid,
The world is like a staircase,
Which the people in poverty need to climb.
It's all down to thinking you're better!

Andrew Leigh (14)
Walbottle Campus Technology College, Walbottle

I Have A Dream . . .

I have a dream that world peace will come about
I have a dream that the bullied stand up and shout
I have a dream that racists should be shot
I have a dream that whales aren't thrown in the pot
I have a dream that discriminators are crushed on the floor
I have a dream that there are no more wars
I have a dream that they are thrown out the front door
I have a dream that there is no more poverty
I have a dream that they all own a property.
I have a dream that there is no more disease
I have a dream that it is cured with ease.
I have a dream that there is no more poaching
I have a dream that the poached aren't left roasting.
I have a dream!

Michael Black
Walbottle Campus Technology College, Walbottle

I Have A Dream . . .

I have a dream, that religions don't fight,
Your skin colour doesn't matter, whether you are black or white.

I have a dream, that there is no pollution,
Poverty is ended because someone found a solution.

I have a dream, that terrorists are gone,
Assassins and abusers know they are wrong.

I have a dream, that blind people have sight,
And homeless people can sleep well at night.

I have a dream, that everyone is treated the same,
Down to what you wear, and even your name.

I have a dream, that smoking is banned,
And there is no litter in the sea or on the sand.

I have a dream that there are no tears,
There is nothing to run from and no one has fears.

This is what I dream.

Holly Taggart
Walbottle Campus Technology College, Walbottle

I Have A Dream

I have a dream:
Where England will lift the World cup in Germany
Where Newcastle will win the Champions League
Where there will be no more murders in the world
Where there is a home for everyone
Where discrimination no longer exists.

I have a hope:
That knives are banned
That the England cricket team will regain the Ashes
That the England rugby team will with the Six Nations
That everyone's dream will come true.

Liam Stewart (14)
Walbottle Campus Technology College, Walbottle

My World Of Dreams

My dream is for a perfect world,
A world with zero poverty.
My dream is for a perfect world,
Where there's no such thing as AIDS.

My dream is for a perfect world,
Where racism doesn't exist.
My dream is for a perfect world,
With no stereotypes on the streets.

My dream is for a perfect world,
Where crime is just unknown.
My dream is for a perfect world,
Where terrorism is gone forever.

This world is nothing like my dream,
It's getting worse and worse.
This world is nothing like my dream,
My dream still waits to come true.

Robbie Soulsby (14)
Walbottle Campus Technology College, Walbottle

I Have A Dream!

The World Cup is coming home
David Beckham will hoist it high
The cup shall be shown in a case all alone
When Wayne Rooney is looking at the sky.

Rooney will score a hat-trick in the knockout stages
We will beat Ecuador by many goals
Every Englishman will be making lots of sound
And the Ecuadorian will be hiding in their souls.

Rooney came back from a broken foot
And we beat Trinidad 2-0
Many of his teammates got bruises and cuts
But it's all worth it to win the final. .

Gavin Smith (13)
Walbottle Campus Technology College, Walbottle

I Have A Dream

I have a dream:
that poverty is banished
that all the homeless have homes
that the rich share more
that everyone is equal.

I have a dream:
that racism is dead
that there are no problems between black and white
that sarcastic racist remarks don't exist
that we all live at peace together.

I had a dream come true:
that bullying is not tolerated in schools
that bullies get punished
that the victims aren't scared to get help
that at least one of my dreams comes true.

Sammiejo Straker (9)
Walbottle Campus Technology College, Walbottle

I Dream

I dream for a world where there are no wars.
I dream for a world where cancer is no longer.
I dream for a world where people don't commit crime.
I dream for a world where everyone has no fear at all.
I wish for a world where everyone is the person they want to be.
I wish for a world where there is no conflict.
I wish for a world where crime is no more.

James Clark (14)
Walbottle Campus Technology College, Walbottle

I Dream

I dream of a world . . .

Where families do not worry about where their next meals will come from, or how far they will have to walk to get water, either clean or dirty water. Parents will not have to watch their children starve or slowly die, knowing that there is absolutely nothing they can do to prevent it. Even babies cling to life by a single, thin thread. Life doesn't have to be so hard. I dream of a world where poverty does not exist.

A place where robberies are not committed, people do not steal from one another because of jealousy of possessions that people have earned through their own hard work and effort. Grudges shouldn't upset friends and families like they do. People who do not have a conscience or feel guilty after doing something which is wrong, simply don't exist. I dream of a world where crime does not exist.

A place that is happy as well as content. The atmosphere is calm, relaxing and fun to be in. Favours are done willingly and open-heartedly, presents are given as a token of appreciation and as signs of love. Sharing is common. I dream of a world where love exists.

A community is united and comforting, yet it is still exciting. Laughter as well as love fills the air. Fights are extremely uncommon, at night there is no noise as everyone sits peacefully in their houses. I dream of a world where peace exists.

With no poverty and crime, the world is a much better place, consisting of mainly two things, love and peace. I dream of a perfect world. But nobody is perfect.

Jasmin Allan (13)
Walbottle Campus Technology College, Walbottle

My Perfect Dream For My World

My dream for a perfect world:

My dream is for nations to stop racism
and for there to be no bullies.
Where children can live clean and peaceful lives.
Where they can stay safe and away from drugs.

A perfect place:
Where clean water is for everyone.
Where countries that are poor have food.
Where we don't harm and pollute the environment.
For innocent people to have a life instead of being shot dead.

A world where:
Nature is not cut down and for it to be like God.
Where children and animals don't get abused like slaves.
Where hate changes to love.
Also for war to change to peace.

A planet where:
Countries can unite and become friends.
For people to not be judged for their looks but their personality.
Where the land looks bright not dark.
Where dolphins swim in the sapphire sea,
Happily without getting caught.
Where for once, everyone can speak and be heard.

This is my dream, is it yours too?

Colin Logan (14)
Walbottle Campus Technology College, Walbottle

I Have A Dream . . .

I dream for a perfect world . .
Where there can be no poverty,
everyone has an equal share of wealth.
Where there is no racism,
the whole wide world is like a big family.
Where there will be no stereotyping,
From Blackpool to Brisbane.
Where there can be no wars,
Fighting is unknown.

I dream for a perfect world . . .
Where everyone can be loved,
With a whole family around them.
Where every person has a home,
A steady shelter above their head.
Where there will be enough food
For you and me to share together.
Where there will be enough medicine
To care for all the sick people all over the world.

Our world isn't perfect . . . this is just a dream!

James Henderson (14)
Walbottle Campus Technology College, Walbottle

I Have A Dream . . .

I have a dream . . .

Where everyone can't stand the waiting,
Where everyone from one country unites.
Where, no matter where you're from, you start debating
Beneath the glow of the floodlights.

I wish in the dream . . .

That the team will achieve,
The greatest honour they can accept,
That they make the other fans leave
And make them have cried and wept.

I hope in the dream . . .

That England will gain,
The golden cup that stands so proud,
That the fans go insane,
Sing, jump, and shout out loud.

Andrew Bainbridge (14)
Walbottle Campus Technology College, Walbottle

My Dream

My dream
Is for England to lift the ultimate prize
With Germans bowing before our eyes
To see the look upon their face
Would be a treat for any race.

My dream
Is for Newcastle to win the Champions League
For Newcastle to beat
The world's elite
My dream is to play for the Toon
And give the fans what they want.

My reality
Is that this won't happen
The world will never see us share,
My dream should be a better one,
Kids are starving,
The world is melting.

We all wish reality was our dreams
But we never wish for a dream reality.

Aaron Rook (14)
Walbottle Campus Technology College, Walbottle

Live Your Dream!

Our perfect world is often spoiled
By immature fools
They all think they are something else
By breaking all the rules.

If only life was better
If only wrong became right
Everyone could live their life
Disabled, black or white.

Everyone is perfect
We all deserve the best
Everybody has a dream
No different from the rest.

So don't be like the others
Who are less than colourful
Every time you have a dream
Live it to the full.

Matthew Thompson (14)
Walbottle Campus Technology College, Walbottle

We Dream . . . It Over!

As we leave the school gates,
They're still there, they all point and shout,
It leaves us wondering what this is all about.
For now though, we all go home, they're still making us feel scared.
We just stare and think, what would happen if they cared?
As everyone parts we look back on today's events,
Wondering why it's us that get all the torments.
We all start to move, checking our backs,
Because we all know how sharply they attack.
We all want to know, why all the name-calling and hurt?
It's not our fault we weren't so alert.
Each time they come near us, we run and try to hide,
Showing that our fear cannot be pushed aside.
We all can't help but feel forsaken,
Well wouldn't you if your life had been taken?

Hannah Richardson (14)
Walbottle Campus Technology College, Walbottle